GOD'S WILL
MADE CLEAR

GOD'S WILL
MADE CLEAR

Written and illustrated
by
MRS. PAUL FRIEDERICHSEN

MOODY PRESS
CHICAGO

Over 75,000 in print
ISBN 0-8024-3040-6

Printed in the United States of America

INTRODUCTION

To you who have accepted Christ as personal Saviour, these chapters are written with prayer that they will encourage you in the Christian life.

Thanks be unto God, that He has made you His child, that Heaven is now your Home, and that you are a joint-heir with Christ. You have been raised to the height and privilege which even the angels cannot attain. It is too wonderful for the human mind! It is a miracle of grace!

No wonder all Heaven rejoices with you because you have been "born from above" on that day when you accepted Christ! It is the most important day in your life, and one that should be remembered with praise and thanksgiving every year, even as you remember your physical birthday. You will spend all eternity thanking God for His salvation and, indeed, it will take all eternity to unfold the greatness of it all.

But in the meantime here on earth, just what can we be and do to glorify the Lord who gave Himself for us? What is His will for us as Christians?

Perhaps the following pages will help to answer some of the questions, and encourage you to live a life that is truly centered on Christ and His will for you.

It would be well that you first read my book, *God's Word Made Plain*, for much that is said here or left unsaid is based upon the surmise that you have read the

5

doctrines of "The Bible, God, the Holy Spirit, Sin, the New Birth, Faith and Works, Souls after Death, Prayer, Sanctification, Eternal Life, Rightly Handling the Word, and Coming Events in Prophecy."

This book is not an exhaustive thesis on any of these subjects, but rather a quick view of the will of God for the Christian, so that you will thirst to drink more deeply of His Word and find for yourself the secret of a happy life—the center of the will of God.

—KAY FRIEDERICHSEN
Wheaton, Illinois

CONTENTS

1

THE WILL OF GOD FOR
JUSTIFICATION

B EFORE WE CAN FULLY UNDERSTAND the will of God for
the Christian, it is well to take another look at the
amazing and soul-stirring meaning of salvation. What
can better impress this on our hearts than the doctrine
of "justification by faith"?

We can understand a loving God who will *make* a repentant sinner righteous; but to realize that our holy
God is willing to *declare* the repentant sinner righteous
(just as if he had always been perfect) is entirely beyond
our ken.

The Bible term "justify" does not mean "to make
righteous," but rather to "declare righteous," or to "reck-
on righteous," to "show to be righteous." It is more than
pardon. A criminal may be pardoned, but he remains
guilty for all that. Justification is far richer than forgiveness. It is to count the guilty not guilty. This is indeed a marvel of divine grace! God not only forgives the
sinner who comes to Him for salvation, but He blots out
the guilt and remembers the past no more! "For I will
be merciful to their unrighteousness, and their sins and
their iniquities will I remember no more" (Heb. 8:12).
"As far as the east is from the west, so far hath he removed our transgressions from us" (Ps. 103:12).

This is one of the proofs that the Bible is the inspired Word of God, for human mind could never invent a holy God who would count me, a guilty sinner, "just as if I'd never sinned!" His ways are higher than our ways and His thoughts are higher than our thoughts! The bill of sin that stands against us is stamped "paid in full" when we accept Christ as our sin-bearer.

We have all piled up a huge debt of sin, but Christ "having forgiven you all trespasses; Blotting out the handwriting of ordinances that was against us, which was contrary to us, and took it out of the way, nailing it to his cross" (Col. 2:13, 14).

It was the custom in Eastern countries to take the paid-up bills of a debtor and nail them to the doorpost to show they were paid. The nails that perforated the bill were proof that they were paid in full. So God nailed His Son upon the tree, and the nails that pierced His hands and His feet were His way of saying to the repentant sinner, "I have paid your debt of sin in full!"

I. Why Do Men Need To Be Justified?

Does this question sound obvious to you? Well, it is not so obvious to many people, for they balk at the indictment that they are sinners and need justification. They feel that they all have something in them that will make them acceptable to God, and will earn them the right to Heaven.

The only answer is to take the Word of God on the matter, and when we do we find that "there is none righteous, no, not one . . . They are all gone out of the way. . . . there is none that doeth good, no, not one. . . . all the world may become guilty before God. . . . there is no difference: For all have sinned" (Rom. 3:9-23). No man is just. None can stand before a holy God and say, "I have no sin; I have not sinned." When we try to say such a thing, we are calling God a liar, for He says we have sinned. That in itself is sin! "If we say that we have no sin, we deceive ourselves, and the truth is not in us. . . . If we say that we have not sinned, we make him a liar, and his word is not in us" (I John 1:8, 10).

When God says: "Thou shalt love the Lord thy God with all thy heart, and with all thy soul, and with all thy mind" (Matt. 22:37), just how many of us can honestly face Him and say "I have done this"? Men have conceived such mistaken ideas about sin and consider some sins as "big sins" and others as "small sins," and yet in the sight of God they are all the same—SIN. God does not grade sin as the farmer grades his potatoes. You know how the farmer does when marketing his crop: the larger potatoes are put together for baking, the next size for

boiling, and the tiny ones he gives to the pigs! But that is just what men try to do with sin: murder and adultery are considered "big" sins, stealing is "medium-sized," but "little white lies" don't count! Yet God says: "For whosoever shall keep the whole law, and yet offend in one point, he is guilty of all" (James 2:10). God is completely holy; not one sin can come before His presence. Jealousy, pride, selfishness, dishonesty, hypocrisy, unkindness—it matters not what it is, as long as it is disobedience to God—it is SIN.

II. How Men Are Not Justified

The sinner cannot be made just by his own efforts, any more than he can lift himself by his own bootstraps. He may increase his education; he may reform his habits; he may raise his social standing and multiply his bank account, but he is still a sinner before God until he receives God's way of justification.

In many pulpits today we have the philosophy, "Do good and be saved!" Or, just as mistaken is the theory that if the good outbalances the bad, then the soul is safe.

A minister actually made this statement recently, "I believe that life is like a balance. If the good you do outweighs the bad, then you will go to Heaven!" But no one can do good before God until he has received the Saviour. All the attempts at doing good are repulsive to God. "All our righteousnesses are as filthy rags" (Isa. 64:6), as long as we are rejecting the Saviour.

IT TAKES MORE THAN A SHALLOW EVANGELISM TO FREE HIM!

FEAR OF PERSECUTION

SINFUL HABITS

SLAVE OF SIN

WRONG RELIGION

Preach good tidings.. proclaim liberty to the captives.. to them that are bound ISA 61.

The sinner cannot be justified by trying to keep some law or code of ethics. To begin with, he cannot keep God's law apart from God anyway, for the very first requirement of God is that we receive His Son as our Saviour. "And this is his commandment, That we should believe on the name of his Son Jesus Christ" (I John 3:23).

There is nothing the guilty sinner can do for himself to wipe the slate clean and count himself as though he had never sinned. Reform will not blot out the sin of yesterday.

"A man is not justified by the works of the law, but by the faith of Jesus Christ" (Gal. 2:16). "No man is justified by the law in the sight of God, it is evident: for, The just shall live by faith" (Gal. 3:11). "By the deeds of the law there shall no flesh be justified in his sight" (Rom. 3:20).

Then why was the law of Moses given? Why bother with something that cannot make the sinner good? "The law was our schoolmaster to bring us unto Christ, that we might be justified by faith" (Gal. 3:19-26). "By the law is the knowledge of sin" (Rom. 3:20). The law was given to show man his need of a Saviour. It is not a means of salvation.

The mirror is an item designed to show us our need of cleansing, but we do not use it to do the washing or the combing! So God's Word says that His law is to show us our sin and make us realize that we are sinners, but the law will not wash that sin away. Only the blood of Jesus Christ cleanses us from all sin.

In speaking to a couple recently about their need of a Saviour, the husband said, "But I feel that I am not yet good enough to be saved. I want to work on it some more."

"Just how good do you think you should be to make yourself eligible?" I asked.

"Well," he wasn't too sure, "I must give up smoking and pay up some debts, and should make things right with my brother-in-law, and—" his voice went on.

"Why, if you are that good, you won't feel you need a Saviour!" I said, "Christ asks that you receive Him to help you be good. No matter how much you clean up your life, you are still worthy only of damnation, because you have not yet received God's Son."

It was a precious time there in that empty church that evening when both husband and wife asked Christ to take their sin away and make them just before God.

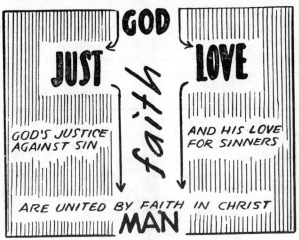

III. How Can Men Be Justified

This is an impossible problem, humanly speaking, for man is *not just!* How can a filthy sinner ever be reconciled to a holy God? God cannot overlook sin; He cannot break His word to punish sin. And yet God is a

God of love. We come to an impasse indeed! How can
the justice and holiness of God ever meet with His love
and mercy to redeem a lost sinner?

There is only one way. That is the way God has provided. His justice demands the death penalty; His love
provides a Substitute. "Be it known unto you therefore,
men and brethren, that through this man (Christ) is
preached unto you the forgiveness of sins: And by him all
that believe are justified from all things, from which ye
could not be justified by the law of Moses" (Acts 13:38).

The whole answer is Calvary!

A. Justification is *provided* through the price for sin
paid on the cross when Christ shed His blood for the remission of sins. "And without shedding of blood [there]
is no remission" (Heb. 9:22). Christ was willing to take
the death penalty that we deserve; to die on the cross as
cursed of God, that we should not have to bear the curse
we have brought upon ourselves: "For he [God] hath

CHRIST IS OUR "PROPITIATION"
(TURNS AWAY WRATH)

made him [Christ] to be sin for us, who knew no sin; that we might be made the righteousness of God in him" (II Cor. 5:21). "Christ hath redeemed us from the curse of the law, being made a curse for us: for it is written, Cursed is every one that hangeth on a tree [crucified]" (Gal. 3:13). "And he [Christ] is the propitiation for our sins" (I John 2:2). The word "propitiation" means to "turn away wrath" or to "placate, or stand between the sinner and God."

B. Justification is *secured* through receiving the Substitute whom God has provided. The moment the condemned sinner accepts Christ as Saviour, then the wrath of God hits Christ and is turned away from the sinner. We are accepted with God because we are *in Christ*. The remedy for sin does no good until we *receive Him*. "Being justified freely by his grace through the redemption that is in Christ Jesus: Whom God hath set forth to be a propitiation through faith in his blood . . . that he might be just, and the justifier of him which believeth in Jesus. . . . a man is justified by faith without the deeds of the law" (Rom. 3:24-28). "Therefore being justified by faith, we have peace with God through our Lord Jesus Christ" (Rom. 5:1).

IV. When Is the Sinner Justified?

The crowning act of God's grace is made possible and becomes a blessed fact to all who are *in Christ Jesus*. "There is therefore *now* no condemnation to them which are *in Christ Jesus*" (Rom. 8:1). Because Christ is sinless and perfect, the obedient believer is made "complete in him." God beholds us as in His Son, and is well pleased with all in Him.

The moment a man admits his sin, throws himself upon the mercy of God and receives the Son of God as his

Saviour, then the grace of God can be applied. The word "grace" means "love in action," or "undeserved favor"; it is the love of God poured out upon the unlovely sinner. Justification is a free gift. He can have it *now.* He enters into the state of peace with God immediately.

Turn with me to the first chapter of Ephesians, if you will, and let us see something of what it means to be *in Christ.*

Ephesians 1:3: "Blessed us with all spiritual blessings . . . *in Christ.*" Our blessings of eternal life, of peace with God and the peace of God, of His presence with us in life and trouble and joy and death, are because we are *in Christ.*

Verse 4: "He hath chosen us *in Him.*" Before the world was ever formed, God had already chosen us who have chosen Him. He chose us that we should be holy and without blame before Him. Note, it does not say without blame only before the public; but *before God* who can see the innermost recesses of the mind! Such holiness is impossible to achieve by ourselves; it is only ours when we are *in Him*.

Verse 6: "He hath made us accepted *in the beloved*." We do not earn this acceptance with God; He has made us accepted. We have no righteousness of our own even after we are saved; it is all of His doing. The only reason that God can count us just is because we are hidden *in Christ* who is just.

Verse 7: "*In whom* we have redemption . . . the forgiveness of sins." We do not deserve or earn this forgiveness. It is undeserved favor because we are *in Him*. The whole plan of salvation entirely excludes any inkling of man's earning favor with God.

Verse 9: "Having made known unto us . . . his will . . . *in himself*." The will of God for our lives is also wrapped up in Christ and we can only know it when we are *in Him*. Without Him we can know nothing and understand nothing of the Word and will of God, for it is in Christ that "are hid all the treasures of wisdom and knowledge" (Col. 2:3). The ability to understand God's will for our lives and unravel the hidden truth of His good pleasure are all bound up in being *in Christ*.

Verse 10. "Gather in one all things *in Christ* . . . even *in him*." Future events and the culmination of the ages are all centered in Christ. He is the Alpha and the Omega (the *A* to *Z*) of all things. He will be the Judge, the King, the Lord of lords. At His name every knee shall bow, and every tongue shall confess Him as Lord. When we are *in Him* we are secure for all eternity, no matter what judgments come upon the earth. Oh, wonderful Lord!

Verse 11: "*In whom* also we have obtained an inheritance." Our estate and reward in glory are all because we are *in Him*. Even the power to earn a reward, the power to serve Him, the desire to glorify Him; all these are due to His grace and help, and then He gives us an inheritance for what we are because we are *in Him!* This is grace unbelievable! We are joint-heirs with Christ!

Verse 12: "Trusted *in Christ.*" This and this alone is the part of the sinner. This is the act of receiving Him and trusting Him to save and to keep and to satisfy, of committing one's whole self unto Him—the moment of justification. The virtue of faith lies in the virtue of the object trusted. That object is the Lord Jesus Christ Himself.

After all the hundreds of technicians and scientists and mechanics have completed a rocket or space missile, and it stands on the launching pad awaiting the final count down, the whole operation lies dormant and useless until the one switch or button is pressed that fires it off. And so all the power of God to work for us, in us, and through us, is held in leash until the button of *faith* is pressed.

It is then that all the force of almighty God is let loose to save to the uttermost all who come unto Him through Christ. Saving faith is the trust that receives the Saviour.

The result of trust is that we should glorify Him.

Verse 13: *"In whom* ye also trusted." In the preceding verse we have seen the object of our trust, Christ. In this verse we see the steps of trust. First, "ye heard the word of truth," the Gospel of salvation. "Faith cometh by

hearing, and hearing by the word of God" (Rom. 10:17).
This is one of the agents of the new birth, the Word of
God. It is needful to know God's way of salvation if one
is to be saved. True, we do not have to know all the
Bible (we shall never know it all), but we must believe
that we are sinners and need a Saviour and that Christ
alone is the Saviour. This is the first step of salvation.

"In whom having believed, ye were sealed" (literal
Greek meaning). The next step of the act of salvation
is *believing* (receiving) Christ. This involves the will;
we pray and ask Him to save us. This is the meaning of
trust. Then when we receive Christ, the Holy Spirit
comes into our hearts, and we become the children of
God and are sealed *forever* as belonging to Him. God's
seal is His Spirit. His seal can never be broken. Thus we
shall never perish but have everlasting life. It is upon this
guarantee that we base our assurance of salvation. Not
that we are good and deserve Heaven, but He is good and
has promised it to those who trust Him. Our part is to
trust Him; His part is to seal us.

The sealing is the work of God. Once again it is His grace in action.

A young woman asked, "Why do I have so many unhappy things come to me? I am no worse than other people!"

I answered, "The real question is, Why do we have so much blessing come to us, for we are no better than anyone else, and we all deserve only the wrath of God and the judgment of God and eternal Hell!"

"You mean that I deserve all the troubles that come to me and more?" she asked.

"We all deserve only eternal damnation. It is only because of the grace of God that we are not utterly consumed." I tried to be as kind as I could and yet speak the truth.

"Yes, I see," she said. "I guess I should be thankful for any favors and mercies that come my way. I realize that I am not really worthy at all for anything, am I?"

"None of us are!" I could speak from my own heart. "Every breath we breathe and every moment we live is by the grace of God; the promise of eternal life in glory and eternity with Him is all by His grace; the privilege of living on the earth to witness for Him today is only by His grace. How grateful we should be!"

V. The Two Sides to Justification

God's side—the sinner is justified by faith in Christ. The justified sinner is secure in his *standing* before God because he is *in Christ*. He is saved. He is justified *positionally;* he is accepted in the beloved. This is what God has done for us.

Man's side—the justified sinner proves his justification

before men by his words and good deeds in obedience to God. Since he is justified before God, he should also be just before men. His *state* of life should be in harmony with his *standing*. He must show that he is justified by his *practice* (Rom. 4:1-5; James 2:14-24). So we have the two sides to the matter, and both are important.

God's Side	Man's Side
What God does for the believer: Justifies *positionally* in Christ; secures our *standing* in Christ.	*What the believer does for God:* Practices being just because of Christ; lives in a righteous *state* because of Christ.

Both of these are the result of justification.

A. WHAT GOD DOES FOR THE BELIEVER

1. We have peace with God (Rom. 5:1). The enmity between God and the sinner is put away. Instead of remaining a condemned criminal before a righteous Judge,

we become the children of God before a loving Father. Because we have peace with God, we can also claim the peace of God which passes all understanding (Phil. 4:7).

Without Him we have no peace. "There is no peace, saith my God, to the wicked" (Isa. 57:21). Neither will there be any peace on the earth until Christ comes back to set up His kingdom of peace. But the believer may have the peace of God right now, for Jesus said, "My peace I give unto you" (John 14:27). Peace is harmony with God.

One evening while sitting around the campfire with a group of vacationers, we were speaking of the Lord and singing choruses. I had my accordion with me, and was asked to play a number. I began to play with loud, clear chords, when "Wowoooo!" a terrific howling set up behind me! I almost fell off the chair, and everyone jumped in surprise! Then we saw what was the trouble. Right behind me was the camp dog. He had been dozing peacefully until I started to play that accordion; then his peace was disrupted and he set up a protest with loud, weird howls! You see, he was not in harmony with his environment!

So often Christian friends have said to me, "But I don't have the peace you speak about. I've never experienced the rest of heart and joy that the Bible promises to Christians."

The only reason we lose out on the peace and joy available to us is because we are out of step with God. Peace means that we are in harmony with God; or a cessation of hostilities. The Christian is *in Christ*. If we are in harmony with Him, there will be peace. The only thing that can disrupt this harmony and peace is sin. Worry, doubt, unrest, discouragement, frustration, are all sin for a believer *in Christ*. To fully realize the meaning of the indwelling Holy Spirit will melt the circumstances and happenings of the world into nothingness, and we can have peace in spite of events and people and distresses, and we will know peace instead of neurosis.

Every true Christian has *union* with God, through our Lord Jesus Christ; we are members of His Body. This

union will never be broken. But many Christians lose their *communion* with God, and live in a backslidden state. George Mueller put as the first effort of his Christian life to maintain communion with God; and from that communion flowed forth a richer service. Sin in the heart of the believer must be dealt with—judged, confessed and forsaken. Then, abiding in Christ, the life will bear fruit for God (John 15:1-11).

2. We are not condemned (Rom. 8:1, 33, 34). Here again is reason enough for peace of heart. "Being now justified by his blood, we shall be saved from wrath through him" (Rom. 5:9). No matter what happens here on the earth, no matter what sickness and sorrow or persecution or misunderstandings, our name is still written down in Heaven and we have the assurance that we shall never stand before the last judgment of unbelievers, but will reign with Christ forever and forever.

3. We are heirs of eternal life and joint-heirs with Christ. "That being justified by his grace, we should be made heirs according to the hope of eternal life" (Titus 3:7). Notice again that justification is by grace alone. We do not earn our heirship any more than a king's son can earn his inheritance. We are born into the family of God by faith and grace. "And if children, then heirs; heirs of God, and joint-heirs with Christ" (Rom. 8:17). We may not have the riches of the world in our pockets now, nor the popularity of the neighborhood, nor the influence over nations today, but we shall some day! This also should give us a deep peace when the waters are troubled around us.

4. We shall be glorified with Christ. "Whom he justified, them he also glorified" (Rom. 8:30). Because of Adam's sin, we all come under the condemnation of God; so by the righteousness of Christ, we may all come into

justification. "Therefore as by the offense of one [Adam] judgment came upon all men to condemnation; even so by the righteousness of one [Christ] the free gift came upon all men unto justification of life. For as by one man's [Adam's] disobedience many were made sinners, so by the obedience of one [Christ] shall many be made righteous" (Rom. 5:18, 19).

Because justification is effected through Christ, so practical justification is also through Him. Salvation is a gift, and so is victory over sin. Both are free if we desire it. The Christ that can save us from Hell is the same who will save us from the power of sin—*if we want it.*

B. WHAT THE BELIEVER DOES WITH GOD'S HELP

We can never really do anything *for God,* but we "can do all things through Christ which strengtheneth me" (Phil. 4:13). As grace begins in God's love to us, so it ends in our love to Him. "Oh, to grace how great a debtor, daily I'm constrained to be!"

Because God has imputed righteousness to us who are not righteous, and because He reckons righteousness even though we are not yet perfect, then we should desire to live up to this righteousness. The justified believer longs to be worthy of God's trust. "But ye are washed, but ye are sanctified, but ye are justified in the name of the Lord Jesus, and by the Spirit of our God . . ." (I Cor. 6:11).

The faith that justifies is also the faith that produces righteousness. It is not enough to *talk* a Christian life; we must *walk* a Christian life! "As ye have therefore received Christ Jesus the Lord, so walk ye in him: Rooted and built up in him, and stablished in the faith, abounding therein with thanksgiving" (Col. 2:6, 7). From the heart of faith in Christ flows the life of good works done in His name.

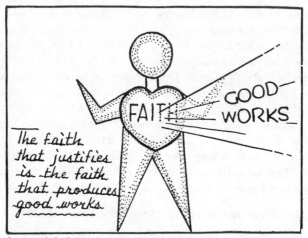

The faith
that justifies
is the faith
that produces
good works

A special friend invited her niece and husband for dinner one evening, and then called me up to "drop by" and try to talk with the husband who was disinterested and rather antagonistic against attending any Bible classes. He was a typical unsaved, worldly man, but the wife was a new Christian. That evening we talked until almost midnight. I used the blackboard and tried to explain the things of God as clearly and simply as possible, hoping to at least arouse the interest of the husband that he might want to know more. We discussed the second coming of Christ, as well as salvation and Christian living, and ended up the evening with explaining how to be "born again." Jim listened intently, and I prayed in my heart that God would speak to him. When I finished the presentation, he said, "Well, that makes sense! I understand what it is all about for the first time in my life. I believe this is what I have always wanted!"

"Then are you willing to accept Christ as your personal Saviour?" I asked.

"Yes, I am!" His answer was clear-cut and sure.

We prayed together and Jim made his first prayer. It moved my own heart. It was clear and simple and yet so sincere that I knew the heart of God and all the angels were rejoicing in Heaven, as another soul was born into the family of God.

When we got up from our knees, there were tears of joy on every face. We talked on for some time, answering questions about how to live the Christian life, and encouraging the couple to get into a sound Bible-teaching church.

Just before it was time to leave, refreshments were served, and I shall always remember Jim sitting there with the cup of coffee in one hand, and the plate of cake in the other saying, "This is my spiritual birthday, isn't it? Then this is my birthday party!"

His small son, who had been going to Sunday school and knew something of the meaning of salvation, was

THIS IS MY SPIRITUAL BIRTHDAY PARTY!

playing in the basement recreation room all this time. But when he came up for the refreshments, his father shook his hand, saying, "Jimmy, this is my birthday. I have been born again. I am saved!" The youngster was amazed and pleased, and hardly knew what to say when his father spoke. All he could say was, *"You,* Dad?"

Each year since that time, Jim has remembered his spiritual birthday. On one occasion I celebrated with him and his wife, and they were a living testimony.

Some time ago, I met them again in a fundamental church in Chicago. They were filled with the joy of witnessing to others and were concerned about giving the right verses to those they were trying to win to Christ. The old life was over, and so were the bad language, the drinking, the worldliness and the sin. Justified and practicing justification too! God bless them!

Lord, make me worthy of Thy trust;
I'm justified!—so make me just.
Thy grace, dear Lord, on me outpour;
I'm sanctified!—so make me pure.

—Kay Friederichsen

QUESTIONS

1. Does God forgive and not forget our sin? (Heb. 8:12)
2. Are there not some good people who do not need to be saved? (Rom. 3:9-23)
3. What is the definition of goodness? (Matt. 22:37-39)
4. Can man be saved by doing good? (Titus 3:5; Eph. 2:8, 9)
5. Will keeping the Ten Commandments save from sin? (Gal. 2:16; Rom. 3:20)
6. Why do we bother with knowing the law of Moses? Why did God give it? (Gal. 3:19-26)
7. Through whom is preached the forgiveness of sins? (Acts 13:38)
8. Why could Christ save us from our sins? (II Cor. 5:21; I Peter 2:22-24)
9. How can we have peace with God? (Rom. 5:1)
10. What does God do for the one who comes to Him for justification? (Eph. 1)
11. What does the one who comes for justification do? Eph. 1)
12. How can one show that he has been justified? (Rom. 4:1-5; James 2:14-24) .
13. Can there be peace on earth before men get right with God? (Isa. 57:21)
14. What is the secret of bearing fruit for God? (John 15:1-11)

15. What is the future of the justified one? (Rom. 8: 30; Titus 3:7; Rom. 5:9)

16. What is the present condition of the justified one? (Gal. 4:7; John 14:27)

17. Who is an heir with Christ? (Rom. 8:17)

18. Who brought the curse of God on the world? (Rom. 5:18, 19)

19. Who can lift that curse and condemnation? (Rom. 5:18, 19)

20. How is a person sanctified? (I Cor. 6:11)

2

THE WILL OF GOD FOR CHRISTIAN LIVING: HOLINESS

Now that you have been justified and have the assurance of Heaven, your chief desire should be to please the Lord who gave Himself for you. All the commands for a Christian can be summarized in six headings: Holiness, Prayer, Bible Study, Worship, Witnessing, Giving. Suppose we take them up one at a time and see just what God desires for our spiritual well-being.

I. Holiness

"As obedient children . . . But as he which hath called you is holy, so be ye holy in all manner of conversation [living]; Because it is written, Be ye holy; for I am holy" (I Peter 1:14-16) .

"Holy" means "free from all defilement, completely pure." This seems a lost subject in a world where men have forgotten that God is absolutely holy, and the fact of sin to a great extent has become a joking matter; also in men's minds the Person of God has deteriorated into a flippant "Man Upstairs," and Satan is a myth.

This callous attitude toward spiritual things, however, does not change the fact that holiness is the paramount attribute of God, and is more often spoken of in the Bible than any other. If a man think well of himself, he has never met God!

Angels and living beings are constantly worshiping Him and saying, "Holy, holy, holy, Lord God Almighty" (Rev. 4:8).

When Isaiah the prophet had a vision of God in all His glory, he heard the seraphim saying: "Holy, holy, holy, is the Lord of hosts: the whole earth is full of his glory" (Isa. 6:3), and Isaiah himself fell down in deep humility and cried, "Woe is me!" He saw himself, and confessed his sin, and was cleansed. The same thing happened to Job. When he saw the character of God, he repented in dust and ashes.

"Exalt ye the Lord our God, and worship at his footstool; for he is holy" (Ps. 99:5).

Because of the holiness of God, He says to us: "Follow peace . . . and holiness, without which no man shall see the Lord" (Heb. 12:14). If only men would believe these words, they might stop and take stock of their lives. Even though we are justified *in Christ,* we want to practice holiness.

In the Old Testament days, God prescribed minutely every detail of His tabernacle and temple, and all was bound up in one theme, "HOLINESS UNTO THE LORD."

And now in these New Testament days, the believers are the temple of God and Christ is our High Priest.

God should not have to tell a Christian, "Do not kill." Instead, He says to us, "Do not hate!" for whosoever hates is a murderer in his heart. He should not have to tell a Christian, "Do not commit adultery," but He says we should not look on people to lust after them, for then we are committing adultery in our hearts.

The commands for Christians are so much more strict than for the unsaved Jews, for we have the indwelling presence of God to enable us to be holy, and they did not.

TEMPLE OF GOD

A. WE ARE TO BE A HOLY TEMPLE

"Know ye not that ye are the temple of God, and that the Spirit of God dwelleth in you? . . . for the temple of God is holy, which temple ye are" (I Cor. 3:16, 17). The temple of God should be as holy and beautiful and useful as He would make it, not only to glorify His name, but also to attract others to love Him.

This should completely dissolve any doubts as to how much sin a Christian can get away with in the sight of God. How sad it is to hear Christians bemoan some pet sin or habit, and complain, "But why can't I do it? What's wrong with it? I want to do what I like!" God answers: "What? know ye not that your body is the temple of the Holy Spirit . . . and ye are not your own? For ye are bought with a price: therefore glorify God in your body, and in your spirit which are God's" (I Cor. 6:19, 20).

B. WE ARE TO BE A HOLY PRIESTHOOD

"Ye also, as lively [living] stones, are built up a spiritual house, an holy priesthood, to offer up spiritual sacrifices, acceptable to God by Jesus Christ" (I Peter 2:5). Every believer is a priest unto God. There is no longer a religious priesthood apart from the believers. Christ is the High Priest (Heb. 4:14-16; 7:24-28; 10:21, 22). If God commanded that His earthly priests be holy in the Old Testament, how much more does He expect that we, His spiritual priests, should be holy! The priests in the temple offered up physical sacrifices, but we are to offer up spiritual sacrifices:

1. "The sacrifices of God are a broken spirit: a broken and a contrite heart, O God, thou wilt not despise" (Ps. 51:17). Repentance for sin is a spiritual sacrifice.

2. "The things which were sent from you, an odor of a sweet smell, a sacrifice acceptable, well pleasing to God" (Phil. 4:18). Giving to the furtherance of the Gospel is a spiritual sacrifice.

3. "Let us offer the sacrifice of praise to God continually, that is, the fruit of our lips giving thanks to his name. But to do good and to communicate [give] forget not: for with such sacrifices God is well pleased" (Heb. 13:15, 16). A life of thanks-*giving* will produce giving!

4. "Present your bodies a living sacrifice, holy, acceptable unto God, which is your reasonable service" (Rom 12:1).

Just what manner of priests are we? Are we fulfilling our ministry?

C. WE ARE TO BE A HOLY NATION

"But ye are a chosen generation, a royal priesthood, an holy nation, a peculiar people; that ye should show forth the praises of him who hath called you out of darkness into his marvelous light" (I Peter 2:9). Our holy Lord has called us to be holy, to be a "special people." That is the meaning of the word "peculiar." We are special for God, in the very center of the circle of His love and grace. God does not ask us to be peculiar—strange, but *special.* It is not glorifying to Him to wear some strange robes or bonnet or quaint dress. By such we are simply drawing attention to ourselves, and that is not godliness.

Our Lord calls us to be holy and to be a special people because He has saved us and lives in us to make us holy. "According as he hath chosen us in him before the foundation of the world, that we should be holy and without blame before him in love" (Eph. 1:4). He never asks us to practice what we can never achieve with His help. True, we are never perfect with sinless perfection, nor is the ability to sin removed as long as we are on the earth. However we can enjoy longer and longer periods of holiness as we allow Christ to rule in our hearts. He longs "to present you holy and unblameable and unreprovable in his sight" (Col. 1:22). "God hath not called us unto uncleanness, but unto holiness" (I Thess. 4:7).

D. WE ARE TO BE A HOLY CHURCH

"That he might present it to himself a glorious church, not having spot, or wrinkle, or any such thing; but that it should be holy and without blemish" (Eph. 5:27). This "church" referred to is the Church universal, the spiritual Church, the Body of Christ, the believers. This is the will of God for us Christians. Housewives can tell us that the way to remove spots is to wash them out, and the way to remove wrinkles is to iron them out! So God washed His "church" with His own blood from all sin, and presses out the wrinkles by the hot iron of discipline, and all for the express purpose that we might

be holy and glorious on that wonderful day when we stand before our Bridegroom, Christ.

"Dearly beloved, let us cleanse ourselves from all filthiness of the flesh and spirit, perfecting holiness in the fear of God" (II Cor. 7:1).

Now we come again to that word "perfect," and it is well to analyze just what it means as far as we are concerned. We shall never have sinless perfection on the earth. That will come when we get to glory and will be like Christ. Neither will we ever be perfect in the sense that we cannot sin, not until we see Him face to face. But that does not mean that we are not going to strive for holiness and experience it too, with the help of the Holy Spirit. After all, it is the indwelling presence of God that enables us to live for Him. The word "perfect" could better be rendered "mature, or full grown," and refers rather to growing in grace and the knowledge of the Lord and to victory and holiness, than to sinless perfection. "To the end he may stablish your hearts unblameable in holiness before God, even our Father, at the coming of our Lord Jesus Christ with all his saints" (I Thess. 3:13).

On that glorious day, the Church will meet the Head—Christ. And the Church will meet the Bridegroom—Christ. Hallelujah! Of the first resurrection, the resurrection of the believers, God says: "Blessed and *holy* is he that hath part in the first resurrection: on such the second death hath no power, but they shall be priests of God and of Christ, and shall reign with him a thousand years" (Rev. 20:6).

After the reign of Christ on the earth, God will dissolve the earth and the universe with fervent heat, and make new heavens and a new earth. "Seeing then that all these things shall be dissolved, what manner of persons ought ye to be in all *holy conversation* [manner of life, conduct] and godliness, Looking for and hasting unto the coming of the day of God, wherein the heavens being on fire shall be dissolved, and the elements shall melt with fervent heat? Nevertheless we, according to his promise, look for new heavens and a new earth, wherein dwelleth righteousness. Wherefore, beloved, seeing that ye look for such things, be diligent that ye may be found of him in peace, without spot, and blameless" (II Peter 3:11-14).

Oh, how unimportant are the things of the world in the light of eternity! And yet how many Christians are quarrelsome, selfish, unkind, completely overlooking the tremendous challenge there is for them to live in peace and love that others might be saved before it is too late! How could any one dicker and yearn over some questionabel worldly pleasure when all these things will soon pass away? How can people live their entire lives for material gain when they will all pass away some day? What a wrong sense of values we so often have! God forgive us!

A certain Christian woman comes to mind in this connection. She was so busy working in her garden and canning vegetables, and weeding, and planting and pruning, and spraying, that she had no time for missionary meetings or church services. She did not need the food, for she had plenty of income; but her cellar was filled with rows and rows of cans of beans and beets and corn and peas. Everyone who visited her had to admire the shelves of canned foods and the grapevines and flower beds before they could get away. Yet, she had no concern for her lost neighbors or for her unsaved husband.

Come harvest time each year she had to empty out some of the jars to can the new harvest! However, she never gave anything to the food shower for a destitute

family, or to a church member who was burned out, or to missionaries home on furlough!

Poor soul! In time, she became so weary from such hard work that she became ill, and then her garden went to weeds and ruin. She was too ill to eat the vegetables in the cellar and they rotted in their juice. She sat day after day in self-pity and her "miseries," and few cared to visit her. Her husband found another woman to interest him. No, she did not have to wait till the old world melted with fervent heat; her world melted right under her nose and she had laid up nothing for eternity or even for a happy old age, except some rows of canned foods and a bank account.

> Dear Lord, give me a sense of values
>   That time and rust cannot decay;
> Help me to lay up holy treasures
>   That will not fade and pass away.

Dear Lord, give me a clear-cut vision
  Of Thee, and things that last for aye;
May I be holy, and selfless: ready
  To stand before Thee on that day!

—KAY FRIEDERICHSEN

QUESTIONS

1. Why should the justified sinner be holy? (I Peter 1:14-16)
2. Who cannot enter Heaven? (Rev. 21:27)
3. What is the occupation of the angels in Heaven? (Rev. 4:8; Isa. 6:3)
4. Who is the Head of the Church? (Col. 1:18)

5. What is the temple of God today? (I Cor. 6:19; I Cor. 3:16, 17)

6. Who are the priests unto God today? (I Peter 2:5)

7. What are the sacrifices offered to God today? (Ps. 51:17; Phil. 4:18; Heb. 13:15, 16; Rom. 12:1)

8. Who are the nation of God today? (I Peter 2:9)

9. What does Christ expect from His spiritual Church? (Eph. 5:27)

10. What is the believer's part in holiness? (II Cor. 7:1; II Peter 3:11-14; Ps. 99:5)

11. When will the Christian be perfect and completely holy? (I Thess. 3:13)

12. Why does man need to be made holy? (Heb. 12:14)

13. Who is the High Priest today? (Heb. 4:14-16; 7:24-28; 10:21, 22)

14. Who are the living stones in the temple of God today? (I Peter 2:5)

15. What is the purpose of being a holy nation? (I Peter 2:9)

16. What was God's purpose for the believer before the world was created? (Eph. 1:4)

17. What is the condition and the occupation of those who take part in the first resurrection? (Rev. 20:6)

18. What will be the end of this world? (II Peter 3:11-14)

19. What is the believer's responsibility in the light of the end of the world? (II Peter 3:11-14)

20. Why should the Christian not live just for the things of the earth? (II Peter 3:11-14)

3

THE WILL OF GOD FOR CHRISTIAN LIVING: PRAYER AND BIBLE STUDY

I. Prayer

PRAYER IS THE HIGHEST EXERCISE in which we can engage, as well as the greatest privilege. Prayer is the slender nerve that moves the muscles of Omnipotence. Through prayer we can reach the whole world.

And yet, how much superstition and ignorance are attached to prayer! It is heart-breaking to see how little men know of God's will on the subject. I remember hearing a prize fighter say over the radio, "I always pray before the fights, so that I will win!" In Spain, it is the practice to say a prayer before rolling the dice in a gambling game, thinking that the Almighty has an interest in all who call upon Him! A woman said to me recently, "I never get what I want from God! Yet the Bible says He will give us the desires of our heart!"

I had to remind her of the first part of that promise: "Delight thyself also in the Lord; and he shall give thee the desires of thine heart" (Ps. 37:4). That makes quite a difference, does it not?

"They that seek the Lord shall not want [lack] any good thing" (Ps. 34:10). No evil, no matter how much

The Ground of CONFIDENCE

This is the confidence that we have in Him, that, if we ask any thing according to His will, He heareth us. —I JOHN 5:14

ACCORDING TO THE WILL OF GOD

desired, will be given. Sometimes the thing we want most and think the best for us might be evil for us from God's standpoint. We should pray that our wishes become merged with the will of God, and then we shall receive what we desire because it is His will too.

"Ye ask, and receive not, because ye ask amiss, that ye may spend it in your pleasures" (James 4:3, A.S.V.).

"And whatsoever ye shall ask in my name, that will I do, that the Father may be glorified in the Son" (John 14:13). This is the secret of answered prayer. When we ask with the desire that God will be glorified, then we will not be dictating our own will, rather leaving it to God to solve the matter according to His will.

There are several qualifications for prayer. Here are a few:

1. Ask according to God's will; that which He would endorse (John 14:13).
2. Ask in faith, believing that God *can answer* (Heb. 11:6).
3. Be sure there is no unconfessed sin to hinder prayer (Ps. 66:18).
4. Do not repeat memorized words that do not come from the heart (Matt. 6:7).

We may ask too earnestly for wrong things, and too languidly for needful things. On the other hand, God says, "Ye have not, because ye ask not" (James 4:2). Prayerlessness is sin not only because we disobey God's command to "pray without ceasing," but because we also hinder the power of God to work in the lives of others as well as ourselves. Nothing can atone for the lack of prayer, for the greatest thing we can do is to pray. We have the generous invitation of our Lord to "come boldly unto the throne of grace, that we may obtain mercy, and find grace to help in time of need" (Heb. 4:16).

Prayer includes more than just the formal church prayer, or even the prayer before meals or at bedtime. Rather it should be our constant thought, moment by moment, hour by hour, "Continue in prayer, and watch in the same with thanksgiving" (Col. 4:2). The "sky

Sky Telegram

telegram" or SOS to Heaven is as important as the time of devotions alone with God each day is important. Make the habit of prayer almost as fixed as breathing. As the Word of God is our food, so prayer is our spiritual breath. We can never take a vacation from prayer. Instead of trying to make your Christian life bend to fit with your secular life, rather bend your secular life to fit in with the spiritual.

Perhaps the best time for Bible study and prayer is the first thing in the morning, so as to prepare for the day ahead. This has been called the Morning Watch, for we take time to watch and pray that we enter not into temptation. What more precious way to begin the day than to look into the face of the Lord! The Christian on his knees sees more than the philosopher on tiptoes!

Oh, but you do not have a place to be quiet alone!

A dear friend of ours is a very godly woman who desired to spend an hour each day in earnest prayer. But when she got up in the morning an hour early, she felt sleepy and drowsy and missed this sleep all day. If she tried to spend the hour at night she again grew weary and sleepy, and the benefit of the hour was lost.

She solved the problem by committing the matter to the Lord. That night she woke up at midnight. She rose and spent an hour in quiet and peace with her Bible and in prayer; her heart was refreshed and warmed. She went back to bed and slept until her usual rising time. That whole busy day was blessed by the quiet hour she had spent at midnight!

From then on she awoke at midnight regularly, spent her hour with the Lord, and never missed the lost hour of sleep!

No man is greater than his prayer life. The pastor who is not praying is playing. The people who are not praying are straying.

"But how do I spend the Morning Watch?" someone might ask.

1. Find a quiet place alone with your Bible. Stop first to ask guidance as you read, then read at least a chapter from the New Testament and one from the Old, each day if possible. Pray as you read. Ask God to make clear the difficult passages; ask Him to help you obey the commands; pray for forgiveness where you have failed in the past; just talk to Him as to a loving father.

Remember the special verses you read and that have spoken to your heart. Try to "pigeon-hole" them in your mind so you can use them to help others. This is the way to begin witnessing—know where to find and apply the verses that have meant something to you.

2. Make a list of persons and requests that you have on your heart, and pray for each one daily. The more you pray, the more you have to pray about!

A friend asked one day, "What in the world would I pray about for an hour? Why, I'm all prayed out in five minutes!"

Try praying for everyone you know and make the requests specific; then watch how God begins to work in those lives. Prayer changes things, and people—including you!

3. Claim the promises of God as you pray. Remember, though, that the promises for prayer are made to believers and not to all men. This is where so many superstitions are started, for men claim the promises of

prayer when they have no right to them. Note the context of each promise and see to whom it is speaking. If we obey God's commandments, He will listen to us. "And whatsoever we ask, we receive of him, because we keep his commandments, and do those things that are pleasing in his sight" (I John 3:22).

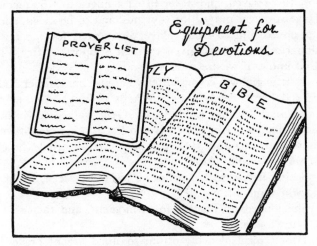

Look at some of these promises, and memorize and quote them as you pray.

"If ye abide in me, and my words abide in you, ye shall ask what ye will, and it shall be done unto you" (John 15:7). We can ask what we will, because it will be His will if we are in close fellowship with Him. Instead of dictating to God as to how to solve our problem, we would do better to lay the matter before Him and ask Him to work it out. He will! Our part is to abide in Him and allow His word to abide in us.

"The Lord is nigh unto all them that call upon him, to all that call upon him in truth" (Ps. 145:18). Our part is to pray with sincerity, and God's part is to draw nigh unto us. So often we pray for that which we do not really care too much about, and we pray because we think it is the thing to do and it eases our conscience. Have you ever prayed for your pastor, and then gossiped behind his back? Have you ever prayed for the lost to be saved, and never lifted a finger to win them? Have you ever prayed for your husband to be saved, and not loved him to God? Have you prayed for the missionaries, and never given to their support? After all, God knows if we are sincere or not.

A little girl was crying bitterly because her mother had denied her a candy bar. She kept wailing, "I want a candy bar! I want a candy bar!" As she walked down the sidewalk, her crying grew less and less and her complaint more indistinct until there was only a half-hearted whine, "I want—I want—I want—!"

Seeing her tear-stained face, a passer-by asked, "What do you want, little girl?"

She looked up blankly for a moment, and then said, "I—don't—know!"

How typical of many of our so-called urgent prayers! There is no sense in always telegraphing to Heaven for God to send a cargo of blessing unless we are at the wharf to unload it when it comes!

"Call unto me, and I will answer thee, and show thee great and mighty things, which thou knowest not" (Jer. 33:3). God's command is to "Call!" He can do more than we can imagine. "Now unto him that is able to do exceeding abundantly above all that we ask or think" (Eph. 3:20). Do not limit the power of God by telling Him how to answer. After all, He can work out a better solution than we can!

"And this is the confidence that we have in him, that,

if we ask anything according to his will, he heareth us: And if we know that he hear us, whatsoever we ask, we know that we have the petitions that we desired of him" (I John 5:14, 15). The key to seeing answers to prayer is to "ask according to his will." Lay the matter before him and sincerely desire His will no matter what it might mean to you, and when the answer comes say, "Thank You, Lord!" The answer might not be what you would have chosen, but it will be better than you might have chosen!

REAL PRAYER IS ALWAYS ANSWERED

He asked for strength that he might achieve; he was made weak that he might obey.

He asked for health that he might do greater things; he was given infirmity that he might do better things.

He asked for riches that he might be happy; he was given poverty that he might be wise.

He asked for power that he might have the praise of men; he was given weakness that he might feel the need of God.

He asked for all things that he might enjoy life; he was given life that he might enjoy all things.

—SOURCE UNKNOWN

Can God still work miracles?

God has never changed. His power is the same yesterday, today and forever. He can do everything and anything, and still does, when it is necessary. But God does not do unnecessary miracles. Miracles were given in the first century to prove the deity of Christ, and then to prove the authority of the apostles (Heb. 2:3, 4). Today

we have the New Testament, the written Word of God, and through it God speaks to man rather than through unusual events and happenings or visions and voices and miracles. The need for miracles has changed, but not the power of God to do *anything*.

Then is the age of miracles over? Indeed not! Where they are needed, they are still seen. If anyone ever saw and believed in miracles it would be the foreign missionary, where superstitious heathen so steeped in darkness and sin would only turn to God when they saw some sign or wonder.

Just for example, a verified account of a missionary and his son in China tells of their efforts to reach a faraway tribe with the Gospel. On their way through the mountains, they were taken captive by murderous bandits and dragged to the courtyard of their chief. The missionaries told the bandits of their peaceful mission to take the message of the God of Heaven to the backward mountain tribe. This only infuriated the rebels the more, and their chief commanded the firing squad of fifty sharpshooters to line up in readiness, as the two missionaries were stood before a courtyard wall.

Praying silently, there was nothing more the godly men could do to help themselves. They believed that God had called them to take the Gospel to the tribes. Was it all to end like this within the next few minutes?

The bandit chief gave the order to load the guns. Then his commands barked out, "Ready! Aim! Fire!" There were a series of clicks—click, click, click! Every trigger was pulled, but not one single gun fired! In surprise and disgust, the rebels shot their guns into the air, and they went off perfectly!

With anger, the chief again shouted his orders, "Ready!

Aim! Fire!" Fifty triggers clicked, but not one gun went off!

By this time, the whole band was decidedly agitated, and some were fearful. With a final effort at command, the bandit chief shouted again, "Ready! Aim! Fire!"

Nothing happened!

Then the frightened men followed their leader as he fell down before the missionaries and begged to hear the message of the God of Heaven. They pleaded with the foreigners to remain with them and be their missionaries. In time, the two men of God traveled on again to the tribes they had started out to reach, and this time they were escorted in safety by the very men who had tried to shoot them!

Miracles? Oh, yes! When they are needed!

Today there seems a movement to seek for miracles, but merely for the personal benefit of the seeker, for some bodily healing or selfish need. Seldom is the desire for miracles based on a burden for the salvation of souls. In fact, there is a teaching in some groups that if you are saved you should never be sick; that healing is included in the atonement, for God "healeth all thy diseases." Certainly it is God who heals! But He has not promised any unnecessary private miracle, and He certainly has not promised that we shall never be sick. Just the opposite. Even the apostle Paul pleaded with God for his physical ailment to be removed and the request was denied; he was instead given grace to endure (II Cor. 12:7-10).

If it were God's will that we should never be sick, then we should never grow old, and would never die! How ridiculous! The Scripture speaks of old age and infirmities and that "it is appointed unto men once to die." If healing were in the atonement, then no Christian should ever be sick, have an accident, lose a tooth, or have gray hair, or die!

Some think that the greatest mircale of all would be the raising of the dead. But even if the dead were raised, they would have to die again! Is that such a great blessing? Lazarus was raised from the dead to show the glory of God, and that the Jews would believe that Christ was God. Jesus said to His disciples: "Greater works than these shall ye do; because I go unto my Father" (John 14:12). What could be greater than the raising of the physically dead? Why, the raising of the spiritually dead, of course! How much greater is it to save a soul from eternal death than to bring back a human body to live a few more miserable years here on earth!

Do not forget, too, that Satan can work miracles; especially during the last days in preparation for the reign of the Antichrist. Satan will give miracle power both to him and his false religious leader. The seeking for miracles today is in preparation for the coming of the miracle-man, Satan's Christ (II Thess. 2:9-12; Rev. 13).

Too often the emphasis on healing of the body through prayer, to the exclusion of medicine or physicians, is simply brought about by a "tightwad" spirit of not wanting to spend money on doctors, rather than by faith in God. Who created drugs? Who gives the wisdom to use them? It is all from God. Luke was a physician. God does heal, but very often His healing is done through the use of the mediums He has created. God does heal, even without means, but He has not promised to heal every case. He does not perform unnecessary miracles. Nor is His healing power limited to certain men or women, or certain "healing meetings," or special methods, or blessed objects, etc.

So-called "healing meetings" or "healers" have some

benefit at times because so many human ills are caused by neurosis, and some plain psychology will snap the person out of it. The same effect would be brought about by any psychiatrist who applied the right therapy. So-called Christian Science is neither Christian (for it denies almost all the basic doctrines of the Word of God), nor scientific (for it denies that there is any sickness or death, and yet claims to have the remedy for both), but it has some simple psychology that any sane and sensible person should know enough to apply. True Christianity has all the basic truths of psychology, too, *but*—and there is a difference—it has the indwelling Holy Spirit, the Spirit of power, to apply the mental therapy *to believers,* if we would only let Him.

The power of God is available to every child of God—to heal, to give victory over sin, to give power to our witnessing. We need not go to some special place or some special person or perform some special ritual. He is *in us* now.

The phrase is so often quoted, "The prayer of faith shall heal the sick." Do not forget, however, that it is the one who does the praying that should have the faith. This is where the "healers" miss the point. They claim that the ones they pray for should have the faith! This makes an easy way out when they have no success in healing. But if healing is to be according to the faith of the one who prays, then self-appointed healers should heal *all!*

Always it is well to take the context of any Scripture verse claimed in any formation of theory. Turn if you will to James 5:14-20.

"Is any sick among you? let him call for the elders of the church." In Old Testament days, the priests were called upon to pass judgment on the sick and to pronounce a man a leper or not. In the early Church Age, the godly leaders of the church assembly, who were the overseers of the flock of God, were to go to the sick. Note, the sick were not taken to the church or to the elders!

"And let them pray over him, anointing him with oil in the name of the Lord." Why the oil? Remember the good Samaritan who used oil and wine for the wounds of the man along the wayside? Wine was used as a disinfectant, and oil as a balm. The oil is also used in Scripture symbolically to represent the Holy Spirit. But

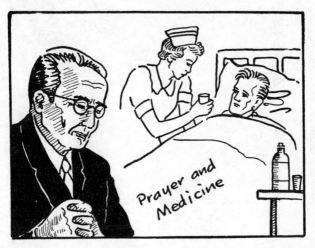

Prayer and Medicine

in this case, however, the person who was sick was a Christian and already had the Holy Spirit, so they certainly were not applying the Holy Spirit! From the context, it seems clear that the oil was mentioned simply to show that after prayer *the physical remedy of medicine was to be applied.*

It also seems evident that the sick person in this passage is a Christian who has sinned and his illness is a re-

sult of God's discipline. This tallies with I Corinthians 11:29, 30, and is dealt with in a later chapter in this book under the subject of "The Judgments."

In James 5:17, 18, the application refers back to the times of the wicked queen, Jezebel, and the drouth that came upon Israel as a result of idolatry. This judgment was not removed until the prophets of Baal were destroyed, *then* Elijah prayed and the rains came. So closely is healing in this passage connected with confession of sin, as well as with prayer and medicine, that there can be no mistake that it is certainly not teaching the modern pattern of healing by means of laying on of hands, or the use of blessed handkerchiefs. Rather is it teaching that Christians who are out of fellowship with God should confess their sin, pray, and apply the available remedy, and trust God to heal. It is always God who does the healing whether with or without the means of medical science, but we can sometimes answer our own prayers by using the common sense that God has given us.

One man who made it a practice to pray that God would save his neighbors, but never lifted a finger to witness to them, was rebuked by his small son one day.

"Daddy," he said, "I wish I could talk like you can."

"Why?" asked his father.

"Because than I could answer your prayer and help save Mr. and Mrs. Webster!"

It is not faith, but presumption to expect God to work a private miracle for us when we refuse to use the means and mind He has put at our disposal.

I know a dear Christian who is too frail to leave her house. But for many years she had been a prayer-warrior for hundreds, yea, thousands, and when she was able she never missed a prayer meeting no matter where it was held. She had little of this world's goods and lived frugally. All she could do was pray. But that is the most important thing that anyone can do! Her prayers are a simple talk with her heavenly Father, and to listen to her is a sermon in itself. You go away feeling you have been truly in the very throne-room of God.

Oh, dear Christian, give God a chance to work through you in real prayer! "The effectual fervent prayer of a righteous man *availeth much*" (James 5:16)

II. Bible Study

The Bible is not just a book: it is *the Book*. When compared with this Book of books, the best of the world's literature pales into nothingness. Other than the records of early Chinese dynasties (1000-1500 B.C.) and the history of Herodotus (5th century, B.C.) we have no written record of world history than given in the Bible. Written world history would be incomplete without the Bible.

And yet it is very painful and humiliating to admit the fact that few books seem to be less known and more hated than this Book of inspiration. Men talk about religion, discuss theories and doctrines, but they often have very little knowledge of what God has said on the matter. Just because they know a few Bible stories and have read the Sermon on the Mount and Psalm 23, some think they know the Bible.

The Word of God is not just a collection of jewels, where one might be more beautiful or more precious than another, but it is a living plant where each part has its particular function, and the entire whole is organically connected, so that no part can be removed or any new part added. It is important to know *all* the Word,

THE BIBLE:
God's
living plant

and to know which part is for whom and about what in order not to drift into error.

The fact that the Bible is the inspired Word of God should be reason enough for us to desire to read and study it. But even beyond this is the actual command of God when He says, "Study to show thyself approved unto God" (II Tim. 2:15). Not to study is to be unapproved of God! Jesus Christ commanded: "Search the scriptures . . . they are they which testify of me" (John 5:39). It seems strange when Christians say they love the Lord, and yet they have no appetite for His Word. It would be as strange for a girl to say she was in love with a young man, and yet never read his letters!

Remember back to your courting days? I can well remember when my sweetheart was away that we wrote to each other almost every day. Such long letters they were, and filled with nothings and yet everythings to us! When I received my letters from *him*, I would read them over and over again, and then keep them under my pillow just to feel him near me. You know how it is! But why all this ado over letters? Because I loved the writer! (Oh, yes! If you are wondering, I married him!)

Love letters!

The Word of God is our love letter from our heavenly Father, from our Bridegroom, the Lord Jesus Christ. Prayer is our love letter back to Him.

Is the Bible our delight, our joy, our daily diet, our life itself? Why not? This is the real test of how much we love Him. One who neglects the Word can never be a success in the Christian life. I have never found a backslider who was reading and studying the Bible.

Instead of growing in the knowledge of Christ through the study of His Word, too often Christians remain babes, weak and sickly, and need to be spoon-fed with the milk of the Word by the minister or Christian worker, instead of taking the bread of life and meat of the Word for themselves. "For when for the time ye ought to be teachers, ye have need that one teach you again . . . and . . . have need of milk, and not of strong meat. For everyone that useth milk is unskillful in the word of righteousness: for he is a babe. But strong meat belongeth to them that are of full age . . ." (Heb. 5:12-14) .

"..Such as have need of milk, and not of strong meat.."

THE OLD BABY !

A. How to Use the Bible

One way *not* to read the Bible is to open it blindly and read whatever is on the page. You might as well do as an American soldier did in France. He went into a French restaurant, picked up the menu, put his finger on the first line that he happened to strike, and ordered, "Give me that."

He got a bottle of pepper sauce! It might be good for its purpose, but was not very nourishing as a meal!

1. Own a good print Bible and a concordance. A Scofield Reference Bible is a good choice, for it has many helps and notes and is a commentary in itself.

2. Set apart a portion of each day for your reading and prayer. Let your body go unfed, rather than your im-

mortal soul (Acts 17:11). Choose a time when your mind is clearest.

3. Pray for the guidance of the Holy Spirit, the Author of the Book (Ps. 119:18).

4. Begin your Christian life by reading the New Testament books first. Perhaps begin with the Gospel of John, then read the Epistle of John, then the books of Peter, James, Colossians, Thessalonians, etc. The New Testament is not necessarily a consecutive book, so do not think you must read it in order. It is well to read the Old Testament in order.

5. After reading the New Testament, then plan to read a chapter each day from the Old Testament and the New. Read the Book over and over again for the rest of your life. You will never cease to find some new blessing when you read with an open and prayerful heart. You can never out-grow the Bible.

6. Study, not just skim, through the verses. When you come to a phrase that is difficult to understand, make a note of it and ask your pastor about it. Weigh each word. Look up all the references and notes given in the margin.

7. Each time you hear a sermon, look up the verses, and see how quickly you begin to understand the meaning of the Bible passages.

8. Try to memorize at least one verse each day. This will help when you want to give an answer to others, as well as keep your mind from idle thoughts and self-centeredness.

9. Carry a New Testament with you to read in spare moments.

10. With the help of your concordance, look up verses on important subjects such as Sin, Faith, Grace, etc.

B. How to Interpret the Bible

So much depends on "rightly dividing the word of truth" (II Tim. 2:15). Every word is for us to read and to know, but there are some parts that are directly *to us* and *for us* to obey.

Before the death of Christ the emphasis of the Bible is *to* the Jews, *for* the Jews and *about* the Jews. Jesus was a Jew and lived under the old arrangement (the old covenant), the Old Testament. He kept the Law of Moses, met for worship on the seventh day (Saturday), and was Himself the fulfillment of the rituals and sacrifices of the Old Testament. The Book of Hebrews in the New Testament brings this out very clearly. For this reason we do not discard the Old Testament. We find much teaching there that makes the life and work of Christ even clearer because it portrays Him in type, and is definitely for our learning.

However, the fulcrum of all history is the death of

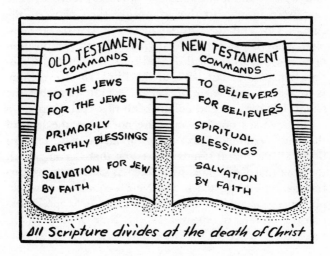

OLD TESTAMENT COMMANDS

TO THE JEWS
FOR THE JEWS

PRIMARILY EARTHLY BLESSINGS

SALVATION FOR JEW BY FAITH

NEW TESTAMENT COMMANDS

TO BELIEVERS
FOR BELIEVERS

SPIRITUAL BLESSINGS

SALVATION BY FAITH

All Scripture divides at the death of Christ

Christ. Here everything in the past is completed, and
everything begins anew. The Old Testament and the
Age of the Law of Moses are ended, and we begin a new
arrangement (a new covenant), the New Testament.

After the death of Christ begins the specific teachings for the Christians, the Church Age. And this Christian way of salvation and living is especially given in the
Book of John and on through the Book of Jude. The
Gospel of John was written about A.D. 90 and is the new
approach that is brought forth by the inspiration of God
through the apostle Paul. Matthew was written to the
Jews that they might recognize Christ as the King. Mark
was written to the Romans that they might see Christ
as the Strong One. Luke was written to the Greeks to
present Him as the Learned One. But John was written
to believers that we might know Him as the Son of God.

The Book of Acts is the account of the deeds of the
apostles and disciples after Christ returned to Heaven,
and we find many miracles and wonders recorded there
that were unique to that transition time between the
Age of Law and the Church Age. The rest of the New
Testament books are letters written by the inspiration
of God to reveal the will of God for salvation and Christian living. The last book of the Bible, the Revelation,
is to a great degree prophecy, and vividly describes the
Great Tribulation and culmination of world history.

Since we are not Jews and are not under the laws of
the Old Testament, that does not mean that we shall
break all the moral standards written there. You see, all
the laws that God wants us to keep as Christians are carried over and repeated in the New Testament, so we do
not have to wonder which ones are for us to keep. Unless
a truth or law is repeated in the New Testament directly for Christians, we know that it has served its pur-

pose and is no longer in effect today. Keeping this principle in mind will help to interpret the Bible.

So you can see that the road to success in the Christian life is clear enough. Shall we take it? Even though the truths of these chapters might be familiar to you, are you practicing them?

God commands that we study His Word. To disobey is sin.

It is always a joy to me when I am invited to a home to explain spiritual truths to interested inquirers. To sit around the table, and with pencil and paper and the Word of God to answer the questions of hungry hearts is nothing short of Heaven itself. The Bible has the answers.

On one such occasion, a husband and wife had invited their friends. For three hours we explained the things of God. It was one of the gentlemen who exclaimed, "Why, it's been right here in the Bible all the time! Why haven't I known it before?" That night four of those present accepted Christ as personal Saviour and are now active in a Bible-preaching church.

Another afternoon, after going through the truth of salvation with a woman of another faith, she exclaimed, "How simple and clear it all is! Oh, that I had known these things long ago, what a difference it would have made in my life, and the life of my family!"

Again, it was the husband of a Christian woman, who was seeking the answer for his spiritual need. He asked questions and listened for some hours, and then could contain himself no longer. He blurted out, "Why, oh, why, didn't someone come to me sooner with this? I am old and gray-haired now, and my life is almost over. What might I have done for God if I had only known the truth before!" That man is now burdened for his family, and is a living testimony for the Lord.

Yes, there is one sure way of breaking up the inroads of error and wrong teaching, and that is to gather around the Book of God. It works 100 per cent every time! Thank God for His miracle Book! Christians, let us use and love and obey it!

I had to learn this lesson in the hard way, however. It was while on the mission field in the Philippines, and my husband was busy in meetings in another town, that I was left in charge of the evangelistic campaign in the town where our house trailer was parked. The priest of the village knew that the missionary man was away, so he took advantage of the situation to send questions to be answered from the platform each night. He did not sign his name to the questions and they were typewritten, but we guessed they were coming from him.

I was in a quandry! I realized that I did not know my Bible too well, and each day I worried over what questions might be asked the next night. I spent the days in prayer and Bible "cramming," just in case he might ask this or that or something else! The whole prestige of the Gospel message was at stake, as well as the honor of the Lord. The questions were brought to me each night as the meeting started, so there was no time to prepare.

I became so concerned, and prayed that the Lord would stop those questions somehow. The next day one of the Christians came to me. He had the questions for that night!

He had found the original list on a table in the provincial building where the only typewriter in town was kept. The list was in longhand and signed by the priest.

Well, that night when the typewritten list was given me, I could answer with great skill! But afterward, I took out the original paper and said, "Friends, I have here the original list of questions that were written and signed by your priest. Each night he has been sending these questions. So if your own priest does not know the answers and must send to me to find the answers in the Bible, now you know that you can trust the Book of God for your problems too. You can safely come and learn of this Book of books!"

That took care of the problem for me too. No more questions!

But it taught me a lesson I shall never forget.

III. How to Have a Family Altar

Nothing will keep a family together like gathering around the Bible each day. The children will early learn to sit quietly and look forward to this special time when Dad and Mother explain the things of God and pray with them. This should be a family time of worship, and not just a mother-and-children time! Husbands are often very insistent to be the head of the house in money matters and plans, but when it comes to the spiritual things, they push it over to the wife and children! The head of the house should be the head of the spiritual training, as well as head of the pocketbook!

When children are very young, it is proper that the mother should take special time to tell them Bible stories and teach them to pray, but that should not take the place of the family gathering. Even though the youngsters might not fully understand the actual reading of the Bible, it is well that they hear it. If the words are explained to them they will soon learn to understand the Scriptures and will not flounder like so many adults who complain, "I can't understand the English of the Bible!" If their parents had read and explained the words to them as children, they would have no trouble as adults in reading the English.

Sometimes it is helpful to have some Bible study book on the children's level to read together, but even this should not take the place of the Bible reading. We sometimes underestimate the comprehension of children. Certainly if they can follow some of the jibberish shown on television and the lingo of the Western movies, they can learn to understand the pure wording of God's Word. At least give them a try!

Prepare the passage you are going to read ahead of time, so you will know how to explain it. Make this part of your own personal devotions. Take turns in reading and leading in prayer. Sing a hymn or a chorus together. This long-lost practice of singing together could well be revived. The importance attached to this time together around the Word of God will mold the lives of the youngsters as they grow up, and prepare them for sitting quietly in church.

Perhaps one of the most precious examples of this worship time is a family in the Philippines who have many mouths to feed. But they realized that there were also hearts to feed. Every morning before breakfast the whole family met around the table with songbooks and Bibles. They sang together, quoted a verse apiece, then read a passage with each child taking his turn. Some read easily and well, others haltingly, and the smallest one read after his mother, but they all took part. Prayer was a simple conversation with God. These children have all grown up to love the Lord and are in training for Christian service and Christian leadership. Thank God, for such parents! How about your home? What sort of emphasis do you place on this special time each day?

Some day will you have to stop and wonder, "Why didn't my children grow up to love the Lord?" It might be that you failed in this precious privilege of the family altar.

When asked for some Bible study course for family worship, I recommend my book, *God's Word Made Plain,* for many have written that they are using it in their homes with success.

Do not neglect this precious time of togetherness with your family and God.

QUESTIONS

1. Will God always give us whatever we ask in prayer? (Ps. 37:4; Ps. 34:10)
2. Why do we not sometimes receive the answer we request? (James 4:3)
3. What should be the motive for prayer? (John 14:13)
4. What right do we have to pray? (Heb. 4:16)

5. Should we mention our request just once and then drop the subject? (Col. 4:2)

6. What will assure answers to our prayers? (I John 3:22; John 15:7; Ps. 145:18)

7. Can God really do *anything?* (Jer. 33:3; Eph. 3:20)

8. Did God always answer "yes" to all the apostles' prayers? (II Cor. 12:7-10)

9. Which of the Ten Commandments are repeated in the New Testament? (Matt. 22:36-40; Acts 15:20; James 5:12; Eph. 6:1; I Peter 4:15; I John 3:15; Matt. 5:28; Eph. 5:5; Eph. 4:28; Eph. 4:25; Col. 3:5; Eph. 5:3)

10. What testifies of Christ? (John 5:39)

11. Who are babes in Christ? (Heb. 5:12-14)

12. Will God hear the prayer of sinners? (Ps. 66:18; Isa. 59:1, 2)

13. What one prayer will God hear from sinners? (Luke 18:13, 14; I John 1:9)

14. What hinders prayer in the Christian home? (I Peter 3:7)

15. Is there advantage in repeating over and over again the same words in prayer? (Matt. 6:7)

16. Is it wrong for a Christian to pray in public? (Matt. 6:5, 6; John 11:41, 42; Acts 27:35)

17. What makes it impossible to please God? (Heb. 11:6)

18. Does God appreciate the prayers of those who do not read and heed His Word? (Prov. 28:9)

19. Can we pray and be heard when we hold a grudge? (Mark 11:25, 26)

20 Is there advantage in united prayer? (Matt. 18:19, 20)

4

THE WILL OF GOD FOR CHRISTIAN
LIVING: WITNESSING, GIVING

I. Witnessing

THERE ARE MANY SCRIPTURAL WAYS to witness for the Lord: by our lips, life and baptism. All three are imperative, for all are commanded.

Searching the Word and soul-winning go hand in hand, just as eating and exercise must go together. So learning of the Lord and laboring for Him should be balanced. Some Christians are overfed and dyspeptic spiritually. They sit in church, read their Bibles, listen to radio sermons, but make no effort to give out what they know. Before long they become critical and hard to live with. The Christian evangelical is often a Christian on ice; but the Christian evangelistic is a Christian on fire!

Others are overzealous but have little knowledge, and zeal without knowledge is a dangerous thing. They sometimes do more harm than good.

Begin your Christian witnessing by giving your testimony and passing on the blessings you have received, but do not let it stop there. "But sanctify [set apart, enthrone] the Lord God in your hearts: and be ready always to give an answer to every man that asketh you a reason of the hope that is in you" (I Peter 3:15). The reason we can

SOUL-NEGLECTING ICE-OLATION OR SOUL-SAVING VISITATION

give the right answer is because God is enthroned in our hearts, and we are so saturated with His Word that it fairly oozes out at every opportunity. The thirsty world around us needs the water of life, the Lord Jesus. He is sufficient for all, but so few know Him. Jesus stood and cried: "If any man thirst, let him come unto me, and drink. He that believeth on me, as the scripture hath said, out of his belly [innermost being] shall flow rivers of living water. (But this spake he of the Spirit) " (John 7:37-39). You and I have believed; we have come to Him and partaken of the water of life, *now* God expects that from us shall flow a constant source of living water to meet the needs of others. This is the natural step after salvation: to want others to be saved.

Recently, a young couple, who had been attending my Bible classes, stayed after the lesson one night to seek salvation. They had been raised in religious circles, but had never known God's way of salvation. They were religious, but lost.

Immediately after their conversion that night they became burdened for their family and neighbors. They spoke to those close by and wrote to those further away. They stirred up quite a hornets' nest over their heads, but they were undaunted. Skeptical and argumentative questions were fired at them, but they would call me up to get the answers before trying to reply.

How rapidly that dear couple grew in grace! They joined a fundamental church and took active part in soul-winning efforts. The more they witnessed, the more they realized they did not know; the more they knew the more they wanted to know! Thank God for them!

Another Christian lady uses her business office as a means of reaching souls. Another, her contacts as a saleslady; a lawyer places his law practice second to witness-

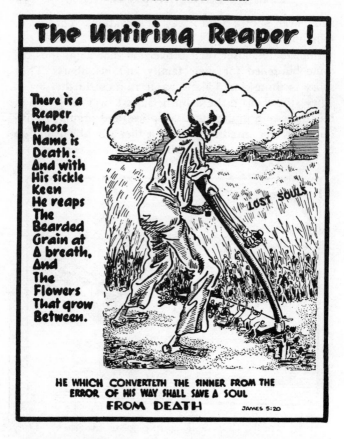

The Untiring Reaper!

There is a Reaper Whose Name is Death: And with His sickle Keen He reaps The Bearded Grain at A breath, And The Flowers That grow Between.

LOST SOULS

HE WHICH CONVERTETH THE SINNER FROM THE ERROR OF HIS WAY SHALL SAVE A SOUL **FROM DEATH** JAMES 5:20

ing to souls. Praise God for such converts! How Heaven must rejoice over them!

Souls are lost *now,* not just some day. The Lord Jesus looked out over the group of Samaritans as they came to Him from the city after hearing the testimony of the woman at the well, and He said, "Say not ye, There are yet four months, and then cometh harvest? behold, I say unto you, lift up your eyes, and look on the fields; for they are white *already* to harvest" (John 4:35) .

Someone has said, "The road to Hell is paved with good intentions." It is also true that the lost may end up in Hell because of the good intentions of Christians who meant to witness some day, but never got to it. Right now the lost are on their way to Hell, and there is no guarantee of tomorrow for salvation. "Behold, now is the accepted time; behold now is the day of salvation" (II Cor. 6:2) . This applies to soul-winning as well as to accepting Christ. We cannot bank on tomorrow. To-morrow may never come.

Even as I write, I am interrupted by a couple at the door. Yesterday I spent several hours with them explaining the things of salvation, but before we could come to the moment of decision, a carload of relatives drove up and I felt it wise to exit as gracefully as possible. I was crushed, for I feared that the opportunity might not come again. But, praise God, here they are now.

How wonderful that God has given them a tomorrow, and they leave now with the assurance of salvation and a radiant smile of joy on their faces.

New Christians, come out from a halting, compromising, hesitating spirit! Do not let your mind be tossed about by conflicting influences and doctrines. Do not be afraid of a little persecution and ridicule. It is good for you! God says that He will honor them that honor Him.

Why is not a believer taken to Heaven the moment he is saved? Because he has work to do for God—a testimony to bear for the Lord Jesus that others might be saved. It is through His people that God has chosen to do His work of love on earth. He has chosen us, mere earthen vessels though we are, to carry the water of life to a world dying of thirst. What a privilege!

But is it not possible to be a good Christian and still not be a useful Christian? The trouble is that an amiable disposition or benevolent emotion is sometimes mistaken for goodness. A child of God who is disobeying the great commission to "go ye into all the world, and preach the gospel to every creature" (Mark 16:15) is certainly not "good."

Disobedience to God is sin. The believer, who is able to witness and is not doing so, is only a refined case of selfishness! It is not enough that we "cease to do evil," we must also "learn to do good."

The Lord, whom we serve and whose name we bear, went about constantly doing good and came to seek and to save the lost (Luke 19:10). It was His meat and drink. He asks us to have the same vision and burden. "Now then we are ambassadors for Christ, as though God did beseech you by us: we pray you in Christ's stead, be ye reconciled to God" (II Cor. 5:20).

This commission is binding upon every believer. Like a radio transmitter, we are to receive the message and broadcast it to others. Our conversion is just the beginning of a life of taking Christ to hearts where He is not known.

But some of us complain that we are not fluent speakers, or we are timid and shy, or have some physical ailment that makes witnessing impossible. Well, we are dealing with a God who knows our limitations and our abilities, and He knows if our complaint is really a reason or an excuse. We must give account to Him.

Not too long ago, two workmen were trapped underground in a cave-in while working on an excavation. Friends and helpers gathered to help dig them out, and anxious families stood near and prayed. After a long tense hour, one man was freed alive. His first question after first aid had been administered was, "How is Jim?"

Learning that his friend was still trapped in the hole, he shook off detaining hands, and grabbed a shovel and joined in feverish digging. All the time he kept calling, "Jim! Jim! Are you all right?"

Two hours later Jim's lifeless body was recovered. But the man who worked the hardest and the most earnestly was the one who had himself been delivered from the horrible death of being buried alive.

Can we, who have been delivered from eternal death in the lake of fire, ever be content to relax in self-content-ment and self-complacency, when we know that others are still doomed without God and without hope? We do not need to know *all* the answers, nor be the most fluent speakers, nor the most robust in health. We just need to allow God to use what strength and talents He has given us.

Now we come to a question. How can this challenge to go into the world be reconciled with the command of God to keep ourselves "unspotted from the world" (James 1:27), and the command to "come out from among them, and be ye separate, saith the Lord" (II Cor. 6:14-17)?

The word "separation" is rather unpopular because men do not want to take a stand against anything. It is so much easier to go along with the crowd. But does the word "separation" mean that Christians should never mix with anyone except Christians?

Of course not! Christ Himself ate with publicans and sinners. He came to seek and to save that which was lost. God does not ask us to withdraw ourselves from contact with the unsaved, but He does ask us to keep ourselves from the level of the world. Jesus Christ prayed: "I pray not that thou shouldest take them [the believers] out of the world, but that thou shouldest keep them from the evil" (John 17:15).

In fact, we are commanded to go into the world to preach; we are encouraged to befriend the lost that they might be saved; we are admonished to love others to Christ. Certainly this is not going to be accomplished by hibernating in a monastery or a cell or with some inner circle of Christian friends.

The word "separation" means much the same as "sanctification"—to be set apart for God.

A Christian is to work among the lost, but not to indulge in their sin. There is no danger when a ship is in the ocean; the trouble comes when the ocean is in the ship! We can be active in our community and our country without dabbling in the questionable practices. "And have no fellowship with the unfruitful works of darkness, but rather reprove them" (Eph. 5:11).

Neither should a Christian choose his bosom friends or life companion from among those who do not love the Lord. "How can two walk together except they be agreed?" I know I could not appreciate for a close friend one who did not like my husband or my son. So I choose my close friends from among those who love the Lord as I do.

More on this subject of "separation" is found in the chapter in this book on "The Church."

II. Giving

All that we are and all that we have belongs to God. "What hast thou that thou didst not receive?" (I Cor. 4:7). We have been loaned a certain span of time and talents with which to do the will of God here on earth, and every thought and act will some day be revealed before all Heaven, and we shall be called upon to "give account to him that is ready to judge the quick [living] and the dead" (I Peter 4:5).

We have originated only one thing. That is our sin. Everything else that we have in the world and in Heaven, and all we have power to do, is the gift of God through His grace, and we are merely stewards to do business for Him until He comes back to earth.

A. WE ARE STEWARDS OF LIFE (what we are)

The born-again child of God has eternal life as well as physical life, and both have been given us that we might live for the Lord who died for us. "He died for all, that they which live should not henceforth live unto themselves, but unto him which died for them, and rose again" (II Cor. 5:15).

To give back to Him the strength and very life that **He** has given us is the true goal of every sincere Christian. **It is** as wicked to rob God of our abilities as it is to rob **Him** of our possessions. Why not give to Him the best of **life** instead of waiting until we are all tired out before **coming** to Him in prayer? Why not give Him our youth **instead** of living for our selfish "fling" and sowing wild **oats** in the prime of life, and coming to God when we are **old** and decrepit? No one would think of offering a **bouquet** of wilted posies to a beloved, and yet that is ex- **actly** what young people are doing when they want to **live** for self while they are young and hope God will **accept** their service when they are old.

"Roses of yesterday ready to throw away."

While dealing with a young teenager one night, I was grieved to see him hesitate to surrender his life to the Lord. I asked what was holding him back from becoming a Christian. His answer was heartbreaking.

"Well, I want to have a good time first. If I become a

Christian I will have to be good and give up too much!"

"Just what do you think so important that you would rather have and do than to know you are going to Heaven?" I asked. "I'll write the list here on this paper."

He thought a moment, and dictated the following list:

"I want to fool around. I want to smoke and dance and bum around with the other kids. I want to cut up in school. I want to do what I like."

That was the list! He meant it too, in all seriousness. How my heart wept for his godly mother who was sitting at the table with us!

God asks that we present our bodies a *living* sacrifice, and not a *half dead* one!

B. WE ARE STEWARDS OF TIME (what we do)

"Redeeming the time, because the days are evil" (Eph. 5:16). We have been left here on earth that we might "buy up the opportunities" for God—opportunities to witness, to love, to serve, to worship, to pray and give and go; to be a blessing *and* to receive blessings, all these are the possibilities at our disposal. But, oh, how we waste our time! By doing so, we are also wasting our opportunities to lay up treasures in Heaven. "Now it is high time to awake out of sleep: for now is our salvation nearer than when we believed. The night is far spent, the day is at hand: let us therefore cast off the works of darkness, and let us put on the armor of light. Let us walk honestly . . . not in strife and envying. But put ye on the Lord Jesus Christ, and make not provision for the flesh, to fulfill the lusts thereof" (Rom. 13:11-14).

Hours spent in mere entertainment might have brought eternal glory. If we spent as much time in preparing our Sunday school lesson as we spend in dressing up for church, what a blessing there might be! Statistics have computed that the average Christian spends eight hours a day in working, eight hours in sleeping, one and a half hours in eating, and *ten minutes* a day in prayer and reading the Word of God! What do we do with the other six hours each day? Are we buying up the opportunities for God? "So then everyone of us shall give account of himself to God" (Rom. 14:12) . We are often so busy giving account of our neighbors or of the church troubles that we have no time to take stock of ourselves! What we read, what we enjoy, what amuses us, all these will some day have to stand the scrutiny of God. Just how will we measure up in the light of eternity?

C. WE ARE STEWARDS OF POSSESSIONS (what we have)

Perhaps you have been agreeing with me in what has been said so far. But now some of you will stop nodding in the affirmative, and will shake your heads in violent disagreement. This topic now is one of the sore spots in Christian principles and practices!

But it is true, just the same, that God has loaned us material things to meet our needs while here on earth, and these include food, shelter, clothing and money. Even the ability to earn wages and the possessions that they will buy all belong to God. "Moreover it is required in stewards, that a man be found faithful" (I Cor. 4:2) . This faithfulness includes using what He has given us, as well as giving back to Him the "rent" that we owe Him. "Upon the first day of the week let every one of you [not just the church officers or the faithful few] lay by him in store, as God hath prospered him" (I Cor. 16:2) . You see, it is God who prospers us.

And yet, how many Christians shy away and boil up when they hear about "giving," because their pocketbooks are not converted! Even though they might hear

GOD'S REQUIREMENT OF THE TITHE HAS NOT CHANGED

only one sermon a year on stewardship, they complain that the church is always begging for money! The fact is, that if every Christian were giving faithfully and proportionately, there would not need to be any mention of money at all. God says, "Honor the Lord with thy substance" (Prov. 3:9; Acts 11:29).

When the offering plate is passed, we sometimes put in a mere pittance or even nothing, and feel very smug instead of ashamed. We sing, "My Jesus I love Thee," and give Him a few odd coins when we owe Him $20.00 perhaps.

Knowing our tendency to give too little, the Lord has given us examples, which furnish adequate information as to His will in stewardship, but which some prefer to ignore. The principle of giving goes all the way back to the first book in the Bible. Abraham gave tithes to the high priest (Heb. 7:2) ; the law of Moses decreed that the priesthood live of the tithes of the people. God's order is, first the tithe and then the offerings.

Some of you say, "But tithing is an Old Testament practice under the law of Moses. We are not under the law!"

You are right; we are not under the law of Moses. But remember that all the commands from the Old Testament which God wants us to obey today are repeated in the New Testament. Now take this principle of tithing. Go back to the Book of Leviticus (6:20) , and you will find that the priests who served in the tabernacle and the temple were to live off the tithes of the people. They had no other income, for they were in full-time priestly service. Now look at I Corinthians 9:13, 14: "Do ye not know that they which minister about holy things live of the things of the temple? and they which wait at the altar are partakers with the altar? *Even so hath the Lord ordained that they which preach the gospel should live of the gospel.*" How much clearer does it have to be made?

If under the old arrangement, when there was no abiding Holy Spirit in the hearts of the people, they were required to give one-tenth, how much more should we give today! The tenth is the minimum.

"A tenth of what?" someone asks. "Just how do we figure the tithe?"

It is a tenth of our net income. If we are a wage-earner and have no expense involved to earn our pay check, then we tithe the entire amount. If we are an employer, then we deduct the overhead of salaries of employees and the overhead of rent and materials, etc., and then tithe the take-home pay (before all deductions are taken out!).

Just why do we need to give to God? Does He really need our paltry cash? Is He not the owner of all?

God has chosen to use human agents to do His work and will on the earth. Money is needed to further this work. How can a pastor or missionary give full time to ministering to spiritual needs unless he is supported? How can we have a place of worship without paying for it? How can we have hymnbooks and study materials without buying them? And so it goes. When we give to the Lord's work, we are giving to the Lord. The tithe is the "rent," and we do not begin to "give" until we have paid our rent. The more we give to God, the more He gives to us. Never fear, no one ever out-gave God! When we shovel out, God shovels in, but He uses a bigger shovel!

Suppose at the first of the month you went to your landlord with a package of candy all done up in pretty wrappings. He would thank you for it, and then ask, "But where is the rent for this month?"

You would reply, "Oh, I brought you a gift! Isn't that enough?"

"Why, no," he would protest, "you must pay the rent if you want to live in my house!"

Just offering to God an occasional gift does not cancel our tithe.

"The tithe is the Lord's," and not for any other purpose than actual Christian work and to further the Gospel. The tithe should not go to needy relatives, or secular charities, hospitals or community needs. It should go "into the storehouse," the house of the Lord.

"Bring ye all the tithes into the storehouse, that there may be meat in mine house, and *prove me now* herewith, saith the Lord of hosts, if I will not open you the windows of heaven, and pour you out a blessing, that there will not be room enough to receive it" (Mal. 3:10).

Those who hesitate to give to the Lord will soon find that they are trying to make ends meet wthout His bless-

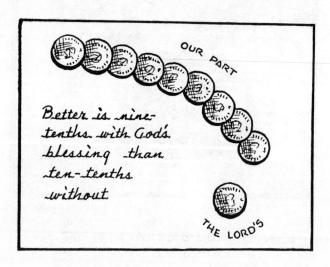

OUR PART

Better is nine-
tenths with God's
blessing than
ten-tenths
without

THE LORD'S

ing. It is far better to have nine-tenths of our income *with God's blessing* than ten-tenths *without!*

The early Christian church shared all things they owned. "And sold their possessions and goods, and parted them to all men, as every man had need" (Acts 2:45). The Christians at Macedonia were commended because in their poverty and persecution they abounded in liberality. Their secret was that they "first gave their own selves to the Lord," and then helped the apostles by their giving. They experienced in reality that "it is more blessed to give than to receive" (Acts 20:35).

It is the motive behind the giving that counts with God even more than the amount. "He which soweth sparingly shall reap also sparingly; and he which soweth bountifully shall reap also bountifully. . . . God loveth a cheerful [hilarious, generous, bountiful] giver" (II Cor. 9:6, 7).

When obliged to be absent from church or a missionary meeting, do not let the cause of God suffer because you did not give. Act from principle, and send your gift rather than hope no one will miss it. Sacrificial giving does not look for a loophole to avoid giving. The motive counts: it is not just *how much* you give, but *how much you have left* that is the real test! Someone gave so you and I might know the Lord; let us then give so others might know Him too.

On the mission field a young convert came to me with a question.

"Ma'am," he said, "just what returns do you get for leaving your home and family and coming out here to suffer persecution and hard work?"

I was taken aback for a moment. But as I looked at him standing there with his glad smile, I had the answer, "You are the 'returns,' young man!"

Can we say with king David: "Neither will I offer burnt offerings unto the Lord my God of that which doth cost me nothing" (II Sam. 24:24)? Or are we instead going to rob God of that which is His due, rob souls of the message of salvation, and rob ourselves of God's blessing?

Can we say with king David: "Neither will I offer

"But my God shall supply all your need according to his riches in glory by Christ Jesus" (Phil. 4:19). Let us trust Him to supply, and when He does, let us trust Him enough to give back to Him the tithes and offerings that we owe Him.

"Charge them that are rich in this world, that they be not highminded." There is nothing wrong with being rich as long as we can be trusted to put God first even in our riches. It is the *love* of money that is the root of all evil, and not money itself. "Nor trust in uncertain riches, but in the living God, who giveth us richly all things to enjoy; That they do good, that they be rich in good works, ready to distribute [give], willing to communicate

[give]; Laying up in store for themselves a good foundation against the time to come, that they may lay hold on eternal life" (I Tim. 6:17-19). It is an old cliché, "You can't take it with you!" But a Christian can send it on ahead!

During an evangelistic campaign in the Philippines, a man came to the local pastor, with whom we were working, and said, "I am willing to join your religion if you sign a paper to say that I will not have to tithe or give to the church."

Poor man, he did not understand that one did not "join our religion," but had to come to Christ for salvation! His theology was as bad as his greed!

I laughingly said to the pastor, "Yes, why not sign such a paper! But it should read like this, 'Although I am using the church paid for by the tithes and offerings of other people, and although I am sitting on a bench paid for by the gifts of others, and although I am using a hymnbook paid for by the gifts of others, and although I am ministered to by the pastor who is supported by the gifts of others, yet I demand that I shall not have to donate anything to the church, and I request that you sign this paper to promise me that I shall be carried along free in your midst as long as I shall need your services.' "

That settled the matter, even for that untaught inquirer!

In sharp contrast, on the other hand, is a gentleman who had a very small salary and a growing family. He learned to love the Lord, and wanted to follow the scriptural principle of tithing. At first he had a battle with his family when he informed them that they would have to do with one-tenth less of their meager income, but he stuck to his convictions. It was not too long afterward that he was offered a better job. Again he stuck to his

resolution to tithe. Again and again his salary was increased. In fact, as the years went by he was so blessed financially that he became the most well-to-do man in the church. His children grew up to love and serve the Lord. I can still hear his testimony ringing in my ears, "How I thank God that He allowed me to learn the blessing of giving when I was a very poor man! Not once since that first decision to trust God with my substance have I regretted my promise. God has never failed me. He truly keeps His promises!"

Too often, instead of trusting the Lord to care for us, we think we can do a better job by ourselves.

The selfish man's poem:

"WE'LL TAKE GOOD CARE OF US, AND YOU TAKE CARE OF YOU!"

O Lord, You know I can't afford to give so very
much;
   You haven't blessed us overly with wealth and
health and such.
If I should give a tenth of all my income, then I fear
   That I could never pay the bills for things I
bought this year!

You see, we needed better clothes (the best is not
too good) ;
   We moved into a better house with acreage and
wood.
I have to have the latest car (I drive to work each
day) ;

   My children need the best of toys for happy,
healthful play.

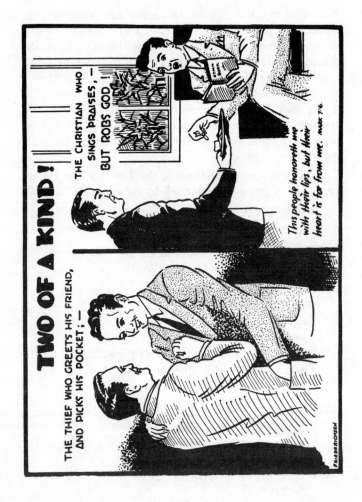

And so our money's used, You see, for useful, needful
things.
Of course, we did spend some perhaps for fun and
trips and rings,
But, Lord, there's really not enough for us and Your
work too;
So we'll just take good care of us, and *You take
care of You!*

—KAY FRIEDERICHSEN

QUESTIONS

1. Why should we witness? (Matt. 28:19, 20; I Peter
3:15)
2. To what does the "water" refer in connection with
salvation? (John 7:37-39)
3. When is the time of harvest for souls? (John 4:35;
II Cor. 6:2)
4. How many souls should hear the Gospel? (Mark 16:
15)
5. What was the mission of Christ? (Luke 19:10)
6. What is the main business of the Christian? (II Cor.
5:20)
7. Does Christ want Christians to be completely apart
from the world? (John 17:15)
8. Then what does it mean to be separate from sinners?
(Eph. 5:11)
9. To whom will we have to give an account? (I Peter
4:5; Rom. 14:12)
10. What should be the goal of every Christian? (II Cor.
5:15)
11. Is the Christian's time his own? (Eph. 5:16)
12. What time is it in God's program? (Rom. 13:11-14)
13. What makes a good steward? (I Cor. 4:2)

14. Upon what day should we bring our offerings to God? (I Cor. 16:2)

15. How do we know that Christians should give at least a tenth? (I Cor. 9:13, 14)

16. Does God bless in accordance with our generosity? (II Cor. 9:6, 7)

17. Can we trust God to supply our needs? (Phil. 4:19)

18. How can a Christian send his money on ahead to glory? (I Tim. 6:17-19)

19. Should we give to God from what is left after we have used all we need? (II Sam. 24:24)

20. What is the first gift that God desires from a Christian? (II Cor 8:1-5)

5

THE WILL OF GOD FOR CHRISTIAN LIVING: WORSHIP

I. Worship

ONE WAY TO KEEP OUR HEART WARM before God is to gather together with other believers for worship and fellowship. You know how quickly a coal taken from the fire will cool off and become dead, and yet when it remains in contact with the rest of the coals it stays hot and alive. So God has commanded His children to come

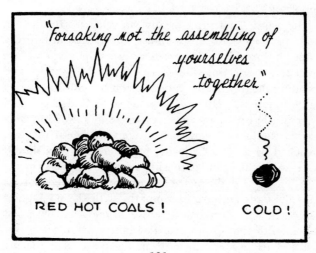

"Forsaking not the assembling of yourselves together"

RED HOT COALS!

COLD!

together for worship. "And let us consider one another to provoke unto love and to good works: Not forsaking the assembling of ourselves together, as the manner of some is; but exhorting one another: and so much the more, as ye see the day approaching" (Heb. 10:24, 25).

The day of the return of Christ is fast approaching indeed, and therefore Christians should more and more desire to come together to exhort each other and provoke to good works. Too often we provoke to anger instead! Or we find that in these last days the churches are cutting down on their services, and believers are staying home on Sunday and Wednesday evenings. If in the time of the apostle Paul the people were willing to spend the whole day listening to the Word (Acts 20), why is it that today when we are so much closer to the return of Christ we seem to think that Sunday morning service is enough for the week, and the rest of the church services are not important?

The word "worship" means "to offer worthship" to God. In order to do this we must ourselves be in "worthy shape" before Him. How can we worship when we are purposely neglecting the place of public worship and spending the day in the country or on the golf links or in family reunions? Direct disobedience to God is sin, and when we have sin in our lives we cannot worship *anywhere*. Radio and television sermons are fine if they are preached by a Bible-believing preacher, but they should not take the place of "gathering together" to worship.

When we attend a place of worship we testify that we are Christians and are in sympathy with the message of the particular church where we attend, and we cast our lot with that group of believers to work together for God. When we stay away from the place of gathering together we must give account to God who can see

WORSHIP ?

through our excuses and will judge us accordingly. No case of "church-itis" will stand up before His scrutiny!

The word "church" means a "called-out assembly" and was applied to the gatherings of faithful disciples after the day of Pentecost. The Church of God is a New Testament institution that will end with the rapture of believers at the second coming of Christ.

At the first, there was but one church gathering in Jerusalem, and James (the relative of the Lord Jesus) was the overseer over true believers. This number was increased and others were added daily as the Holy Spirit worked through the preaching of the apostles.

Later on, because of persecution and scattering of the Christians and because of their missionary vision, the Gospel spread throughout Palestine and then into Asia Minor and Gentile countries around. The local gatherings of the Christians in different towns called themselves

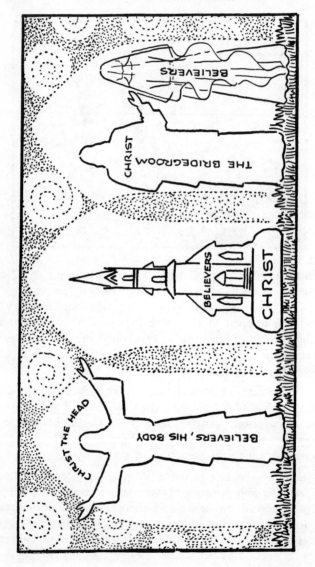

"churches" and they met in homes or outdoors or wherever they could worship unmolested. So it has come to be that the word "church" has now two meanings—first, the "called-out ones," the saved ones, the Christians, the believers, wherever they might be; and second, the local gathering of believers in buildings. Technically, the word "church" should not be applied to a building. The place of meeting should be called a chapel or meeting house.

The Church of God is believers. This is the Church invisible, the Church universal, the Body of Christ, the Bride of Christ, the saints whose names are written down in Heaven.

The local church is the church visible, where the names of the faithful are written on the roster.

II. The Church Universal

The saved ones, the born-again children of God, are all in this universal Church. This spiritual Church is called the "body of Christ," "the church, which is his body" (Eph. 1:22, 23). "And he [Christ] is the head of the body, the church" (Col. 1:18; Eph. 5:23).

The moment we receive Christ as personal Saviour we are in His Church. He is our Head and we are part of His Body. We do not join this universal Church as we would some local organization. We become one with Him by partaking of His life when we are born into His family, and this membership is based upon union with Christ. "And the Lord added to the church daily such as should be saved" (Acts 2:47).

Before the death of Christ there were two classes of people: the Jews and the Gentiles. But now in this Age of Grace, the Church Age, there are three classes of people: the unsaved Jews, the unsaved Gentiles, and the saved Jews and Gentiles—the Church of God (I Cor. 10: 32).

The spiritual Church is also likened to the Bride, and Christ is the Bridegroom. The apostle Paul, through the inspiration of God, says: "I have espoused you to one husband, that I may present you as a chaste virgin to Christ" (II Cor. 11:2). In Heaven we shall meet our Bridegroom and sit down with Him at the marriage supper. "Let us be glad and rejoice, and give honor to him: for the marriage of the Lamb [Christ] is come, and his wife [the believers] hath made herself ready. And to her was granted that she should be arrayed in fine linen, clean and white: for the fine linen is the righteousness of saints . . . Blessed are they which are called unto the marriage supper of the Lamb" (Rev. 19:7-9).

The spiritual Church is also likened to a building that is built upon Christ who is the foundation. "For other foundation can no man lay than that is laid, which is Jesus Christ" (I Cor. 3:11). "Now therefore ye are no more strangers and foreigners, but fellow citizens with the saints, and of the household of God; And are built upon the foundation of the apostles and prophets, Jesus Christ himself being the chief cornerstone; In whom all the building fitly framed together groweth unto a holy temple in the Lord: In whom ye also are builded together for an habitation of God through the Spirit" (Eph. 2:19-22).

This spiritual building is based upon Christ as the *Rock*. He alone is the foundation of the Church. Upon Him are built all the teachings of the apostles and prophets (the Old and the New Testament), and note it says *all the apostles*, not just one! The teachings of the apostles and prophets are the Bible truths as we have them today and have had them throughout the past nineteen hundred years. They have never changed. The stones in this spiritual temple are those who are in the family of God "through the Spirit," and not by deserving deeds. This building or temple is not made with hands. "Howbeit the most High dwelleth not in temples made with hands" (Acts 7:48). Buildings and things are not the dwelling place of God today. He dwells only in the hearts of the believers, His Church (I Cor. 3:16; 6:19).

This is the Church to which Christ referred when He said to Peter: "Upon this rock I will build my church" (Matt. 16:18). Peter had just made the magnificent statement through the enlightenment of the Holy Spirit: "Thou art the Christ, the Son of the living God" (Matt. 16:16). This is indeed the basis of all truth, the foundation of all Christian faith—*Christ is God!*

Christ pronounces a blessing upon Peter for this statement, and then goes on to make clear the comparison between Peter and Himself. There is absolutely no basis to construe that Christ is calling Peter the *Rock*. The very wording of this passage makes it clear in the Greek that Christ is saying:

"Thou art Peter." "Thou" means "you," the second person. "Rock" in this case is "Petros" in the Greek, which is masculine gender and means a "small stone."

"Upon this rock." "This" refers to the first person. "Rock" in this instance in the Greek is "Petra" which is feminine in gender and means a "large boulder."

Christ was referring to Himself as the Rock. Peter also makes this clear when speaking of Christ: "To whom coming, as unto a living stone, disallowed [rejected] indeed of men, but chosen of God, and precious, Ye also, as lively [living] stones, are built up a spiritual house . . . Behold, I lay in Sion a chief cornerstone, elect, precious: and he that believeth on him shall not be confounded"

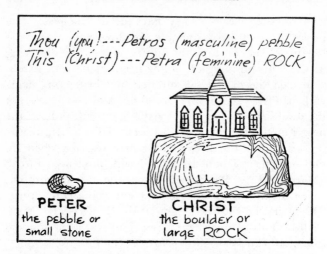

Thou (you)---Petros (masculine) pebble
This (Christ)---Petra (feminine) ROCK

PETER
the pebble or
small stone

CHRIST
the boulder or
large ROCK

(I Peter 2:4-6). "This is the stone [Christ] which was set at nought of you builders, which is become the head of the corner. Neither is there salvation in any other: for there is none other name under heaven given among men, whereby we must be saved" (Acts 4:11, 12).

The apostle Paul too speaks of Christ as the *Rock*. "That spiritual Rock that followed them: and that Rock was Christ" (I Cor. 10:4).

The Bible does not leave us guessing on this score. Peter was simply a "chip from the Rock," if you like, but never the *Rock*. He never went to Rome! Neither did he ever head up any local church!

III. The Local Church

In apostolic days those who belonged to the Lord were included in (the Church universal) the local assemblies. Believers who loved the Lord gathered themselves together for worship, prayer, praise and service for God, and these local gatherings were called after the name of the town, such as the church at Corinth or Galatia or Rome. The apostle Paul founded many of these churches during his missionary journeys, and then would leave some spiritual man to pastor and oversee them. Occasionally, Paul would return to visit and preach, and often wrote letters of instruction to them. He says, "I teach everywhere in every church" (I Cor. 4:17). His greatest burden was not his own persecutions and sufferings, but "the care of all the churches" (II Cor. 11:28, 29).

A. THE PURPOSE OF THE LOCAL CHURCH

1. *To gather together for worship and mutual edification* (Heb. 10:25).

There is something about united effort that encourages. Gathering together to praise God and to study His Word is heart-warming and practical. It would be difficult for each Christian to secure a private pastor and conduct his own personal worship services, so by uniting together and pooling resources it is possible to procure a place to meet as well as trained leaders. This was the apostolic method. Just as we unite to attend a school where one teacher can minister to many students, so we gather together where one servant of God can minister to the whole group.

WHERE WERE YOU?

"I came to your church last Sunday; I walked up
and down the aisle.

I noticed your seat was vacant," said the Master with
a kindly smile.

"Oh, I was at home!" I answered. "Some folks from
home-town way

Dropped in for a weekend visit, so we stayed in the
house all day!"

The Master gazed at me sadly as He was about to
  speak.
"My child," He replied, "are there not six other days
  in the week?"

I saw I had grieved my Master; and slowly as He
  turned away
I vowed He'd not find me absent again on His special
  day.

2. *To evangelize* (Matt. 28:19, 20).

Some think that this Great Commission was given only
for the Jews under the Old Testament dispensation of
Law, but the words read: "Go ye therefore, and teach
all nations, baptizing them in the name of the Father,
and of the Son, and of the Holy Ghost: *teaching them* to
observe all things whatsoever I have commanded you."
"Go ye into *all the world,* and preach the gospel to *every
creature*" (Mark 16:15). Unless the local church is win-

Where were you?

ning the lost to Christ, it is missing its purpose for existence. This does not just mean winning people to the denomination or getting names on the church roll, or even baptizing the church children, but it does mean the actual conversion of the unsaved and the deliverance of souls from sin unto holiness.

3. *To glorify God by holy living and good works.*

These days one finds much emphasis on good deeds toward mankind, but very little emphasis on holiness toward God. Much activity is concentrated on helping the poor, the hospitals, the orphans and war sufferers, but worldliness is rampant, and personal holiness is practically unknown. The church is to encourage and teach practical holiness without which no man may see the Lord.

IV. The Ordinances of the Church

In contrast to the idea of some that there are seven sacraments of the church, and that all spiritual grace must be dispensed through the church, the Word of God teaches only two ordinances and neither dispenses any spiritual grace. To begin with, "grace" means "unmerited favor," and cannot be earned by adhering to any rules or rituals or sacraments.

A. BAPTISM (Matt. 28:19, 20; Acts 8:37; 16:31-34; 18: 8)

Baptism does not help to save a soul. Then what is its purpose?

There are four ways in which the word baptism is used in Scripture. But always the word "baptize" in the Greek means to "immerse, to dip under and come up out of." Even today the modern Greek uses the same meaning for the word. It never means anything else.

1. John the Baptist's baptism (Matt. 3). This was the

baptism unto repentance when John baptized in preparation for the coming Messiah. This was not believers' baptism. After Peter's sermon on the Day of Pentecost the Jews were convicted of having crucified their Messiah, and "they were pricked in their heart, and said unto Peter and to the rest of the apostles, Men and brethren,

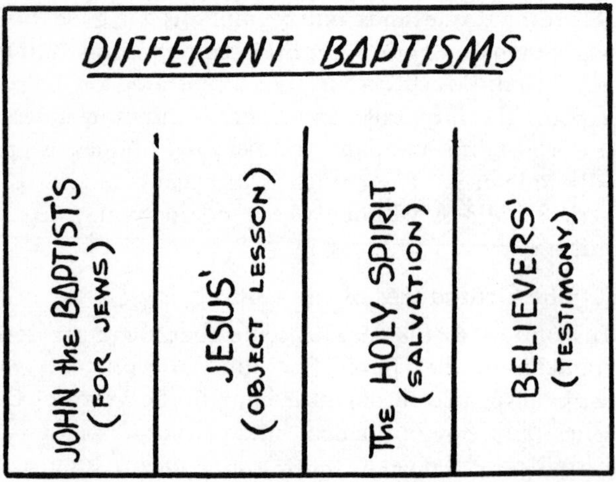

DIFFERENT BAPTISMS

JOHN the BAPTIST'S
(FOR JEWS)

JESUS'
(OBJECT LESSON)

The HOLY SPIRIT
(SALVATION)

BELIEVERS'
(TESTIMONY)

what shall we do? Then Peter said unto them, Repent, and be baptized every one of you in the name of Jesus Christ for the remission of sins" (Acts 2:36-38). Their baptism in the name of Jesus was to show their repentance for the crime of crucifying Him. The baptism did not remit their sins. "For the remission of sins" does not mean "*in order* to have remission of sins," but rather, "*because* of the remission of sins." Just as one might say, "Take your umbrella for it is raining." This does not mean that taking the umbrella will make it rain, but take the umbrella *because* it is raining.

2. Jesus' baptism (Matt. 3). Jesus was baptized to

"fulfill all righteousness." He does not ask us to do anything that He would not do Himself, and His baptism was an example for us. It was a type or object lesson of His death, burial and resurrection. He asks us to follow His example and fulfill all righteousness too.

3. The baptism of the Holy Spirit. The word "baptism" is also applied to the act of salvation. When we receive Christ as our Saviour, the Holy Spirit comes into our hearts and we are "immersed into Christ," into the Church. "For ye are all the children of God by faith in Christ Jesus. For as many of you as have been baptized into [unto] Christ have put on Christ" (Gal. 3:26, 27). It is very clear that when we become the children of God by faith, we are immersed into the Body of Christ. "Know ye not, that so many of us as were baptized into [unto] Jesus Christ were baptized into his death? Therefore we are buried with him by baptism into death: that like as Christ was raised up from the dead by the glory of the Father, even so we also should walk in newness of life" (Rom. 6:3, 4).

In these verses the subject is salvation, not water baptism. Water can never make anyone a child of God. It can never save a soul, nor wash sin away. "For by one Spirit are we all baptized into one body, whether we be Jews or Gentiles . . . and have been all made to drink into one Spirit" (I Cor. 12:13). This baptism by the Holy Spirit is a union of faith and love when we are immersed into the Church universal; it is a spiritual act of receiving Christ.

4. Believers' baptism (Matt. 28:19). "Baptizing them in the name of the Father, and of the Son, and of the Holy Spirit." Water baptism is not an aid to salvation, but it is a testimony of salvation. The whole meaning of the ordinance is to show publicly that we who are saved

have been buried with Christ and have risen to live a new life for Him. The requirement for believers' baptism is first to be a believer! "And many . . . believed, and were baptized" (Acts 18:8).

Just as it is possible to be baptized and not be saved, so it is possible to be saved and not be baptized. Sometimes health or circumstances hinder a believer from following the Lord into the waters of baptism, but that does not change his status as a child of God. The thief on the cross who repented was saved though he was not baptized. On the other hand, Simon the sorcerer was baptized but was not saved (Acts 8:9-24).

Suppose you studied for four years in college and passed all the examinations, then you would be eligible to take part in the graduation ceremonies. But if you were ill and could not be present at the ceremonies, would you still be a graduate? Of course! On the other hand, though, suppose you never studied in college at all, but just put on a cap and gown and joined the grad-

This makes a graduate —

This announces the graduate to others

DIPLOMA
Course — — —
— — Completed

Salvation is by faith in Christ —

Baptism is the public testimony

uation procession, would that make you a graduate? No!

So it is with salvation. We are saved by receiving the Saviour, but the baptismal ceremony is to show to others that we are saved.

I remember a professing Christian couple who wanted to be baptized, but their testimony was so poor and their lives so worldly that the pastor suggested they wait until they could honestly say, "I am crucified with Christ," before they made the public step. The couple was offended and went off to another church where they were not known, and were baptized the next Sunday.

I asked them a few weeks later, "Just what did your baptism mean to you?" They hesitated and then said, "Well, we feel better now!"

"Were you really saved before your baptism?" I asked.

"Yes, I think so," the wife answered, "but we feel more sure now!"

That afternoon I spent some hours with them trying to explain the meaning of baptism, and that the ordinance was simply a public testimony that they were living a new life in Christ. The young couple hung their heads.

"I see it all now," the husband spoke up at last. "How foolish we were to think that baptism might make our salvation more sure! We really acted a lie when we told the world that we were dead to sin and living for God."

"Well," I told them, "the answer is to make right with God and really live up to your testimony now!"

They did. The wife said to me some months later, "How I wish we could be baptized now that we are right with God instead of back there when we did not understand it all!"

"He that believeth and is baptized shall be saved; but he that believeth not shall be damned" (Mark 16:16).

This verse does not say that baptism saves. The last phrase shows that it is unbelief that damns. But baptism is the natural sequence of salvation. It should definitely follow conversion.

"Whosoever therefore shall confess me before men, him will I confess also before my Father which is in heaven. But whosoever shall deny me before men, him will I also deny before my Father which is in heaven" (Matt. 10:32, 33). Baptism is a privilege as well as a requirement, a joy as well as a command.

B. THE LORD'S SUPPER, OR COMMUNION (I Cor. 11:23-34)

The other ordinance of the church is the observance of the Lord's Supper.

Who may take the communion? Those who belong to Christ, to the Church universal, and who are in fellowship with Him. The heart that has been searched and forgiven is the heart that is invited to the Lord's Table. In fact, any unconfessed sin, any unforgiving spirit, any unyielded thought or ambition, will hinder His blessing and bring His discipline. God's will is not that Christians should abstain from the communion when they have sinned, but that they make right and put away sin, and partake of the Lord's Supper!

From the example of apostolic days, the "breaking of bread," or communion, was observed on the first day of the week, or the Lord's Day. It was this day that Christ rose from the dead; it was this day that He appeared to His disciples twice after His resurrection; it was this day that the Holy Spirit came in pentecostal power; it was this day that the disciples met for preaching and the taking up of offerings and tithes. "Upon the first day of the week, when the disciples came together to break bread, Paul preached unto them" (Acts 20:7).

The Lord's Supper is in no way an aid to salvation. It is done to remember the Lord's death "till he come" at the end of this Church Age. He is not physically present today, and yet some believe that when the church bell rings and the special words are spoken or a prayer is offered, that the wafer and cup actually become God; the bread is the flesh, bones and sinews of Christ, and the cup is actually His blood. If this were true, then there would be no need to repeat the ordinance since Christ has already come. After all, when God does a miracle it is recognizable. The water that was turned into wine tasted like wine! But if the wafer and cup do not change into God, then the reverence and adoration given to it is idolatry. Either way, it is wrong according to Scripture.

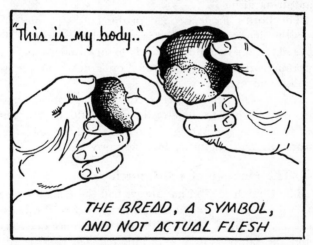

"This is my body.."

THE BREAD, A SYMBOL, AND NOT ACTUAL FLESH

Altogether too much importance is placed upon the physical cup and bread in many churches, and the entire ordinance has become a superstitious ritual. We do not receive Christ into our stomachs, but into our hearts by faith. Just as Jesus said, "I am the vine," and "I am the door," it certainly did not mean that He was physically a vine or a door. He was using a type or illustration.

He was yet alive when He said, "This is my body." Did that mean that He then had two bodies, His own and the bread? When He broke the bread did He have many bodies? If so, then every time the communion is prepared there are thousands of Christs! The whole idea is absurd.

Some believe that by eating the bread and drinking the cup they receive eternal life. Judas ate the bread and drank the cup. Did he have eternal life?

When Christ passed the cup, He said, "Drink ye all of it." This did not mean that one disciple was to drink *all* of it. Rather, that each one was to drink of it. And yet, in some churches the clergy alone take of the cup and drink all of it.

The Lord's Table is open to the Lord's people. To pass the elements to unsaved people is sheer mockery. To give it to small children, who do not understand the meaning of salvation and the Lord's death, is just as foolish and useless.

It is amazing how much error and superstition have become attached to these ordinances of the church, and yet how clear the Word of God is about the meaning, procedure and eligibility for these privileges.

V. The Message of the Church

The Church of God has always had the same message. It is this message that distinguishes it from false teachings and religions. "The faith which was once delivered unto the saints" (Jude 3). This message is called the *fundamentals of the faith.*

Since the time of the apostles, this message has not changed one iota, and there have been no subtractions or additions. These fundamental truths are the basic doctrines upon which the apostolic church was founded, and are the truths we stress in these chapters.

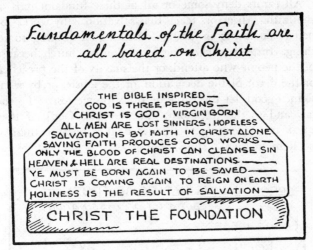

Fundamentals of the Faith are all based on Christ

THE BIBLE INSPIRED —
GOD IS THREE PERSONS —
CHRIST IS GOD, VIRGIN BORN
ALL MEN ARE LOST SINNERS, HOPELESS
SALVATION IS BY FAITH IN CHRIST ALONE
SAVING FAITH PRODUCES GOOD WORKS —
ONLY THE BLOOD OF CHRIST CAN CLEANSE SIN
HEAVEN & HELL ARE REAL DESTINATIONS. ———
YE MUST BE BORN AGAIN TO BE SAVED ———
CHRIST IS COMING AGAIN TO REIGN ON EARTH
HOLINESS IS THE RESULT OF SALVATION —

CHRIST THE FOUNDATION

Here are some of the fundamental truths:

A. The Bible alone is the Word of God. (Not traditions, not dreams of religious leaders, not inventions of new teachings, not the writings of teachers.)

B. God is revealed in three Persons. Jesus Christ is God, born of a virgin, died for our sins, rose again, and is coming again.

C. All men are sinners. There is no good in any; all are without God and without hope.

D. Salvation is by faith in the Saviour alone, by being "born again" by receiving Christ as personal Saviour, and not by baptism or good living.

E. Saving faith will always produce a life of good deeds in obedience to God's Word.

F. Heaven and Hell are literal eternal destinations.

G. A "saved" soul is saved forever.

H. Christ is coming again to the earth to set up His earthly kingdom.

All errors deny some or all of these fundamentals of the faith. All errors teach that salvation is by works—by being something or doing something or joining something. Instead of choosing a religion or church because of the people who attend, or the suavity of the preacher, or the decor of the decoration, or the music, or by what sounds good, let the Bible be the supreme test. "To the law and to the testimony [the Word of God]: if they speak not according to this word, it is because there is no light in them" (Isa. 8:20).

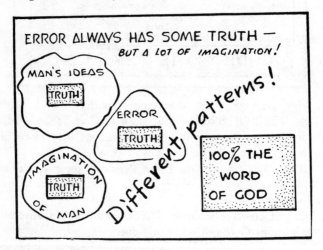

VI. Why Join a Local Church?

"Can't I be a good Christian without joining a church?" The man who asked the question was a fine person, in regular attendance at church, but he just did not want to "get involved" in any church.

"Why, yes," I answered, "you can be a good Christian

without joining a church, just as you can be a good human being without belonging to any country! But you're saying by your attitude that you don't think any church is good enough for you, and you will be a very poor testimony. Some day you might even find yourself like the man without a country, and wish you had some pastor to minister to you and some congregation to care for you."

Why join a church?

A. When you join a church you are telling others that you believe what it teaches. You are casting your lot with those who love the Lord, and are testifying to what you believe.

B. When you join a church you are pooling your efforts and money to do a work for God that you could not do alone.

C. When you join a church you are shouldering some of the load of evangelizing the neighborhood and foreign fields.

D. When you join a church you can expect the love and concern of the pastor and people in spiritual or physical need.

E. When you join a church you have the advantage of the spiritual knowledge that the pastor can give because of his preparation, and the benefits of a place of worship where you can help to safeguard the message.

There are some church tramps among Christians, who prefer to visit around and follow the special attractions and features in each church without having to shoulder any responsibilities. They expect the attention and concern of all the churches, and yet offer little in return. They use the facilities of all the churches, and yet pay for none of them. They drift around sampling all the spiritual meals, as it were, and walk out without paying

the bill! They take advantage of the hard work of others, but do nothing themselves. They criticize the failure of the churches, but never do anything to help alleviate the problem. They are always filling a seat when there is something special doing, but are absent when the attendance is slim and they are really needed. Surely such are not gladdening the heart of God! Their actions simmer down to pure selfishness.

On the other hand, I know one man who never attends church at all because none of them is good enough! He has some complaint against every church in town, and yet there are many fine fundamental churches within walking distance. He cannot get along with anyone, and is always feeling hurt because he is not called on to speak or teach, so he stays at home and says he can worship God better there than in any church!

Not to gather together for worship is disobedience to

God, and disobedience is sin. With sin in our lives **we cannot** worship God anywhere!

WHICH ONE ARE YOU?

Some Christians are like wheelbarrows—not good unless pushed!

Some are like canoes—they need to be paddled!

Some are like kites—if you don't keep a string on them they fly away!

Some are like kittens—they are only contented when petted!

Some are like balloons—full of wind and likely to blow up at anything!

Some are like trailers—no good unless pulled!

Others are filled with the Holy Spirit—thank God for these!

VII. Where Do the Different Religions and Denominations Come From?

Pagan religions are inventions of wicked hearts who "did not like to retain God in their knowledge, God gave them over" (Rom. 1:28).

False cults are sometimes called Christian religions, but are mostly men's imaginations plus a little Bible truth. Error usually rides on the back of truth, so there must be some truth, or people would not swallow it. Usually a leader invents some new idea, and claims to have gotten it from God in a dream or a vision or from some book from Heaven (which subsequently evaporated!). They all appeal to the physical, to the sensual, to the mind, and are not in harmony with the fundamentals of the faith. The only way to discern truth and error is to compare the teachings with the Bible, not just part of the Bible, but *all* of it.

Denominations were mostly founded upon the Scriptures, and differed in their church organization and observance of ordinances. These differences came about to a great degree because of geographical isolation, when little groups in a certain area imbibed a certain emphasis and followed their leaders in perpetuating that particular phase of church doctrine. However, on the way of salvation and the fundamentals of the faith, most of the so-called Protestant denominations were soundly established on the Word of God.

Some churches in the major denominations now, however, have gotten away from the very fundamentals upon which they were founded. The first church was the apostolic church, and there are those who have never gotten away from the truth. But today it is hard to find many churches that are still clear in testimony against worldliness and in the message of salvation.

For the sake of illustration, suppose we take the messages to the seven churches in Asia Minor (Rev. 2:3), and see how closely they coincide with church history from Pentecost up to this day. The description was primarily of those particular local churches, but has also proved to be a prophetic picture of the periods of church history in the Church Age.

A. THE EPHESUS CHURCH (Rev. 2:1-7)

The name of this church means "desirable," and describes the early apostolic church period when the Christian church was true to the Word of God, and the New Testament was given. This line of truth has gone down throughout the last two thousand years without change, and there are those who have never deviated from this line. Let us call this line in the diagram, the fundamentals of the faith, or the fundamental church.

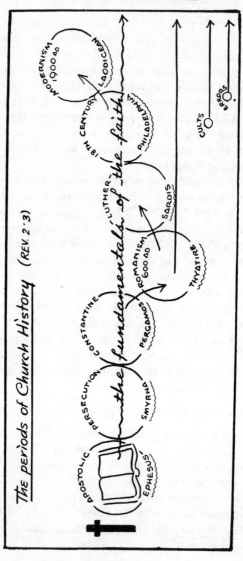

The periods of Church History (REV. 2·3)

the fundamentals of the faith

APOSTOLIC — EPHESUS
PERSECUTION — SMYRNA
CONSTANTINE — PERGAMOS
ROMANISM 600 AD — THYATIRE
LUTHER — SARDIS
18TH CENTURY — PHILADELPHIA
MODERNISM 1900 AD — LAODICEA

CULTS
ERRORS

B. THE SMYRNA CHURCH (Rev. 2:8-11)

The word "Smyrna" comes from "myrrh" and means "suffering." For the next two centuries, the Christian church was persecuted and scattered and the Roman emperors tried to crush it by killing the Christians. Nero especially played a prominent part in this tribulation of the church, and burned martyrs at the stake and threw them to the lions if they would not denounce their faith in Christ. But the church was still on the line of the fundamentals of the faith.

C. THE PERGAMOS CHURCH (Rev. 2:12-17)

Now we see a change. Christianity suddenly becomes popular when Constantine (a Roman emperor) becomes a Christian, and the word "Pergamos" means "married to power," for now the church and the state were united under the one head, the emperor. This worked out all right as long as Constantine was a genuine Christian. But after him came other emperors who were not saved persons, and they still claimed to be the head of the church. From here on comes the break-away from the fundamentals of the faith.

D. THE THYATIRA CHURCH (Rev. 2:18-29)

This period began about A.D. 500 and was a gradual slipping away from the truth into a conglomeration of Christianity, Judaism and heathenism. The very word "Thyatira" means "continual sacrifice," and describes the paramount teaching of the church of Rome; i. e., that Christ dies afresh on the altars of the Roman church each time the Mass is said. Now rituals and superstitions are added to the Bible teaching, and the use of images, relics, and robes take the place of spiritual worship. The fact that they call themselves the Catholic universal church does not mean that they are God's universal church. That name, as well as the name of pope, priest, father, etc., are all self-appointed, and to say "Roman Catholic" is a complete paradox! The claims that the Roman Catholic church was the first church is not only foolish according to the Word of God, but in contradiction to history itself!

From the church history of the Roman church, notice just when some of these religious innovations were introduced:

A.D. 600 Latin used in the churches. Prayers to Mary and the saints introduced.

A.D. 700 The cross, relics and images used as aids to worship.

A.D. 900 Lent and not eating of meat on Fridays.

A.D. 1000 The use of holy water; celibacy of the priests; the use of the rosary.

A.D. 1100 The institution of the Mass; the sale of indulgences (to shorten the term of suffering after death).

A.D. 1200 The bread actually becomes God (transubstantiation), the worship and adoration of the bread; the confessional (confessing sins to the priest).

A.D. 1400 The priest only partook of the cup; the teaching of purgatory (a place of suffering after death where unconfessed sins are burned away by fire. A place where the suffering could be shortened by payments for special prayers)!

A.D. 1500 The Apocrypha books were added to the Bible, and the traditions of the Roman church were placed on a par with the Bible.

A.D. 1800 Mary was sinless. The Pope is sinless while officiating in his capacity as the Vicar of God (the infallibility of the Pope).

A.D. 1900 Mary's mother was also a virgin, and Mary was born of a virgin just like Christ was. This is called the "Immaculate Conception."

A.D. 1954 Mary ascended bodily to Heaven just like Christ did.

The continual invention of new dogmas is the only way the Roman church can keep alive. Now if these teachings were true, do you think God would have waited nineteen hundred years to reveal them to just one church group? Would He not rather have introduced them in His inspired Word? Such a mixture of heathenism and ritualism with very little Christianity is hard to imagine! However, the main fault with the whole Roman system is that their claim for salvation is through the church, through works and the seven sacraments (baptism, confirmation, marriage, confessional, the Mass, penance and the last rites at death). Salvation by *works!* This places that religion where it belongs—with the cults and errors.

This same church of Thyatira is alluded to again in Revelation 17, where it is distinguished as the religion of the city of seven hills, *Rome.* It co-operates with the Antichrist until he eventually crushes it. This church will pass through the Tribulation, and will increase and grow in these last days as one of the signs of the times that Christ is soon to return.

But all through this time, there are still those who have not departed from the fundamentals of the faith.

E. THE SARDIS CHURCH (Rev. 3:1-6)

Now follow the Reformations, the break-away from the tyranny of the Pope. Luther, the Church of England (Episcopal), etc., make an attempt to get back to the fundamentals of the faith. However, they still carry over some of the rituals and practices of Rome, and their form

of worship has remained after the pattern of Rome down through the last century. These groups are really the only Protestants, for they protested against Rome. Other groups which had not gone into Romish teachings have never had to come out of Roman Catholicism.

F. THE PHILADELPHIA CHURCH (Rev. 3:7-13)

This brings us up to about A.D. 1800 when there was a back-to-the-Bible revival in Europe and throughout its colonies. America itself was founded by those who sought to escape the dictatorship of state over church, and longed to get back to the Bible truth in all its purity. This revival period is called the church of "brotherly love."

G. THE LAODICEAN CHURCH (Rev. 3:14-22)

The word "Laodicean" means "self-made" or "complacent," and so adequately describes the period in which we live now. Although the non-Roman churches were stablished on the foundation of the truth, yet today some of the major denominations have gotten off the line of the fundamentals of the faith, and have branched in a new direction of "Modernism," or apostasy. This departing from the faith is anything but modern, for it dates back to the Garden of Eden. It is the age of "humanism," of doubting the Word of God, of denying the faith, of substituting human effort for God's grace, and emphasizing *works* instead of salvation by faith alone.

God speaks of this Laodicean church as being "lukewarm" and nauseating to Him. The people are self-satisfied, rich and self-righteous. They do not realize that in God's sight they are spiritually sick and dead in sins, and they need the healing, saving touch of the Holy Spirit and the covering of Christ's righteousness. The admonition is to *repent!*

Here is one of the most heart-breaking of all pictures: Christ standing outside the door of the church and knocking for admission! He says to the professing church of these last days: "Behold, I stand at the door, and knock" (Rev. 3:20).

This is indeed a picture of Christendom today and tallies with the prophecies of the "last days" when "some shall depart from the faith" (I Tim. 4:1-3). Now as never before, apostasy and Modernism are spreading throughout the Christian churches, and we see the fulfillment of these words: "And many false prophets shall rise, and shall deceive many. And because iniquity shall abound, the love of many shall wax [become] cold" (Matt. 24:11, 12). "This know also, that in the last days perilous times shall come. For men shall be lovers of their own selves . . . lovers of pleasures more than lovers of God; Having the form of godliness, but denying the power thereof: from such turn away" (II Tim. 3:1, 2, 4, 5). "For the time will come when they will not endure sound doctrine; but after their own lusts shall they heap to themselves teachers, having itching ears; And they shall turn away their ears from the truth, and shall be turned unto fables" (II Tim. 4:3, 4).

This is the church period in which we are living right now. It is one of the signs that the Lord is soon to return. At His coming, the true believers, His spiritual Church, will be caught away, and then will be ushered in the Great Tribulation that will come upon the professing churches and the unsaved world alike. All religions will be gathered together at the beginning of the Tribulation to co-operate with the Antichrist (Satan's Christ). We already see this coming to pass in the efforts of federations of churches, etc., and the movement to unite all religions in worship and work, whatever their belief or testimony.

VIII. What Is "Modernism"?

This movement away from the fundamentals of the faith is called Modernism. There are still many small denominations that have not fallen into this doctrine of Satan described in II Peter 2:1-3: "But there were false prophets also among the people, even as there shall be false teachers among you, who privily shall bring in damnable heresies, even denying the Lord that bought them. . . . And many shall follow their pernicious ways; by reason of whom the way of truth shall be evil spoken of. And through covetousness shall they with feigned words make merchandise of you." But in the last seventy-five years or so, most of the major denominations have been swept into this liberal apostasy, some more and some less, until even the seminaries are turning out young ministers, who do not even know the meaning of "being born again," or the "coming again of Christ," or "separation from worldliness." The denominations have become political machines that dictate to the local churches and control the money and the message and the preachers. The decline into this apostate state has been so insidious and gradual that many congregations do not realize where they have drifted. They only know that they do not hear the "good old Gospel" any more.

Just as there are degrees of Communism, such as "pinks" or "reds," so there are degrees of Modernism in the churches, and it is sometimes difficult to know just where the line divides. Many good people in the churches are actually hungry for Bible teaching and salvation, but they do not know where to find it.

There are stages of Modernism. It is well to be able to recognize them.

A. WORLDLINESS IN THE CHURCH. The first sign of decline into apostasy is seen in the letting down of the standards set forth in the Word of God. Drinking, dancing, card parties, etc., are even practiced among some ministers. The methods of raising funds for the church have changed from the tithes and free-will offerings of the Christians to bazaars, lotteries, sales, suppers and soliciting. This is a warning sign that the church is departing from the faith.

B. SOME BASIC TRUTH OMITTED. It is possible to attend some churches for years and never hear clearly how to be "born again," or that all men are hopeless sinners, that God will not hear prayer when there is unconfessed sin in the heart, that we cannot help to save our souls by good deeds. Instead they hear lectures on the power of positive thinking, on world politics, on being a good neighbor and citizen. Now these things are all right in their place, but they do not save souls. Church members are not being taught how to win souls. Instead they believe that there is good in all, and all are the children of God and all will end up with God some day. Sermons are powerless platitudes of fine oratory; prayers are read or recited. This is a modernist church, perhaps the most typical in our American cities today.

C. BLATANT DENIAL OF THE TRUTH. Many leaders of modernistic denominations are to a great degree out and out liberals in theology. Their main theme is the "Fatherhood of God and the brotherhood of man." They ridicule the miracles and explain them away by "circumstances, or feasible atmospheric conditions, etc." They deny the deity of Christ, the virgin birth, the reality of Hell, the authenticity of the Bible. They speak of "the Master" and right living, but have no answer for lost souls because they do not believe there are any lost souls. This is rank Modernism.

IX. God's Answer to This Sad Situation

Throughout all this confusion of error and apostasy, there are those who truly belong to the universal Church, and who still hold to the faith once delivered to the saints! Some of these people find themselves involved in modernist churches without realizing it. Just what are they to do about it?

We are responsible for our connections as well as our convictions. There are two things that are important to a Christian—unity and truth. But if it comes to sacrificing something, it is better to sacrifice unity rather than truth. The things of the truth of God must be held inviolate, no matter what the cost. It is a matter of principles and not just personalities. Too often Christians follow a leader or a friend, and do not analyze the principle in-

volved. It is not a matter of following some popular personality who has been promoted by superpublicity, but rather a following of the principles and practices of the Word of God. God's command to "contend for the faith" does not mean "tolerate error for the sake of peace."

A steward of the Lord must be wise as well as faithful. It certainly is not wise to try to build up a church that is going to tear down as fast as you build. Much better to cast your lot with a group that is holding to the truth and know that you are building on a foundation where the pastor and people will build with you.

For decades, godly men and women have tried to stem the tide of Modernism in their churches and denomina-

tions, but to no avail. There are many good people in liberal churches who do not approve of what has happened to the church, but they are in such a minority that they cannot contend with the political machine of the denomination. So they have given up the effort, and just go along with things as they are and hope for the best. They give their money to the general fund of the denomination, little realizing that they are actually supporting the modernist seminaries and missionaries that are doing so much harm, and abetting the cause of apostasy.

Some such good people feel that they can do some good by staying in their liberal churches. But they eventually find out that their efforts to clean up the worldliness is not welcome, and the message they teach to their Sunday school classes is torn down by the youth director or pastor or parents.

Just what is God's command about this situation? The Scripture is very clear. If the following passages from God's Word are read carefully and prayerfully and with an open mind, there should be no doubt as to what a born-again believer should do about his church connections.

"Now I beseech you, brethren [believers], mark them which cause divisions and offenses contrary to the doctrine which ye have learned; *and avoid them*" (Rom. 16:17, 18). This verse is not speaking of divisions in the church caused by standing for the truth, but by wrong teachings.

"Be ye not unequally yoked together with unbelievers [anyone who does not stand for the truth] . . . Wherefore *come out from among them,* and be ye separate, saith the Lord" (II Cor. 6:14-18).

"And have no fellowship with the unfruitful works of darkness, but rather reprove them" (Eph. 5:11).

"Now we command you, brethren [note that this is a command to the believers!], in the name of our Lord Jesus Christ, that ye *withdraw yourselves* from every brother that walketh disorderly, and not after the tradition which he received of us . . . If any man obey not our word by this epistle, note that man, and *have no company with him,* that he may be ashamed. Yet count him not as an enemy, but admonish him as a brother" (II Thess. 3:6, 14, 15). You see, the only reason for contact with the apostate church is to *admonish* and protest the error.

In case these verses are not clear enough, take a look at this next passage: "Whosoever transgresseth [steps over the line, out of the truth of God], and abideth not in the doctrine of Christ [the whole message of the Word], hath not God. . . . If there come any unto you, and bring not this doctrine, receive him not into your house, neither bid him Godspeed: For he that biddeth him Godspeed *is partaker of his evil deeds"* (II John 9-11).

This is very obvious. To remain in a modernist church or any church that is not 100 per cent on the fundamentals of the faith is to be partaker of their evil deeds!

So many times Christians have said, "Well, I don't believe all they teach, but I like the music (or the ritual, or the people, or the preacher, or something), and so I attend anyway. After all, I can worship God anywhere!"

Can you? Can we really worship God when we are disobeying Him? To blatantly disobey God does not make us eligible for worship.

But there are many godly people who have obeyed the Lord, and have come out from churches that are not preaching the truth clearly, and have had to leave be-

hind their investment of many years in the church building or the work done there, and start all over again from
scratch. That is why so many fundamental churches are
small in comparison to denominational churches.

From most of the major apostate denominations have
sprung up protest groups that have started fellowships of
fundamental churches without the hierarchy of the political machine, and where each local church is an in-
dependent unit free to choose its own pastor at will and
to designate its missionary giving. Some of these Bible-
preaching groups are called the Bible Presbyterians, the
Regular Baptists, the Conservative Baptists, the Fundamental Congregationalists, etc., just to mention a few.
In local gatherings where people from different denominations have united for worship, the name "Bible
Church" is often used. Perhaps all these could be called
the new Protestant churches—protesting apostasy!

For God's blessing, *God's work must be done in God's
way.* We cannot "do evil that good may come" in the
work of the Lord. Do not sail under the wrong flag!

So we get back again to the word "separation" to find
that it applies to connection with the wrong church, as
well as with wrong living. The separated life is the righteous life of the justified believer who desires to be separated from sin, from apostasy and from close fellowship
with the unsaved.

A Christian is warned to marry "only in the Lord"
(I Cor. 7:39). When we disobey this command of God,
we reap by misery and trouble and heartbreak. Parents
would do well to discourage their young people from
even dating unsaved friends. Dating often leads to love
and marriage. It is better to avoid the temptation of
becoming fond of an unsaved person and the possibility
of the unequal yoke (II Cor. 6:14). In olden days God

forbade that two different types of animals should be yoked together for plowing. So He also commands that the Christian and the unsaved should not harness together for life partnership or church service or any other business when there is a choice of companions. The marriage of a Christian and an unsaved person is in direct disobedience to God. It is sin.

A young woman, who was very active in the Lord's work, fell in love with an unsaved young man who had a tendency to drink. Her Christian friends warned her of the danger of disobeying God, but she contended that she was going to reform the man and he would be saved by her marrying him. She was insulted when her pastor refused to marry them, and went to another preacher who did not have strong scruples on the matter. Soon after marriage that girl found that her friends and pastor were right, and God was right too!

Her life became a nightmare. Her husband drank constantly. She had cut herself off from the church group by

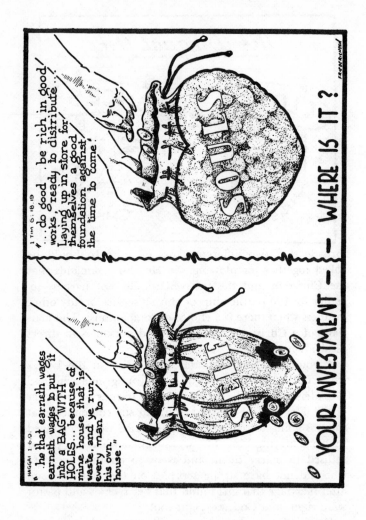

her pride and rebellion and was now ashamed to return. She lived in misery and heartbreak.

She eventually did try to return to the church services, but her husband forbade her to attend. She was broken in spirit.

Many years later when she did brave the wrath of her drunkard husband to go back to church, she was old before her years. She had but one message for the young people, "Don't marry an unsaved person!"

Another young woman comes to mind. She was a fine Christian, a beautiful girl, and a bright prospect as a Bible woman among her own people while she was attending Bible school. Then she married an unsaved man of another faith. When I saw her again after some years, I was amazed at the change that had come over her. She dared not attend church. She had to raise her children in the error of their father. She could not even teach them the truth in secret. She was almost kept a prisoner in her house. She had to buy liquor for her husband when she did the marketing.

Old before her time, she had but one statement to make, "I am reaping for disobeying God!"

QUESTIONS

1. Why should Christians gather together for worship? (Heb. 10:24, 25)
2. Who is in the Church universal? (Acts 2:47)
3. What are the three classes of people today? (I Cor. 10:32)
4. Who is the foundation of the Church? (I Cor. 3:11; Eph. 2:20; I Peter 2:4-6; Acts 4:11, 12; I Cor. 10:4)
5. Why should a Christian submit to water baptism? (Matt. 28:19, 20; Acts 8:37; Acts 16:31-34; Acts 18:8)

6. What is the baptism of the Holy Ghost? (Gal. 3:26, 27; Rom. 6:3, 4; I Cor. 12:13)

7. What is the requirement for believers' baptism? (Acts 18:8; Acts 8:37)

8. What makes a Christian worthy to partake of communion? (I Cor. 11:27-29)

9. How can we tell if a religion is right or wrong? (Isa. 8:20)

10. What are the seven periods of church history? (Rev. 2; 3)

11. What is God's will for Bible-loving Christians who are members of liberal churches? (II Cor. 6:14-18; Eph. 5:11; II Thess. 3:6, 14, 15)

12. What does God command concerning those who do not preach the truth? (II John 9-11)

13. What is one of the signs of the last days? (I Tim. 4:1-3; Matt. 24:11, 12; II Tim. 3:1, 2, 4, 5; II Tim. 4:3, 4)

14. Whom should a Christian marry? (I Cor. 7:39)

15. Why are the heathen lost? (Rom. 1:18-24, 26, 28)

16. At what door does Christ stand and knock? (Rev. 3:14-22)

17. Should a Christian stand up for the truth of the Word of God? (Jude 3)

18. What is the one reason for a Christian to continue in contact with those who do not preach the truth? (II Thess. 3:14, 15)

19. What is the "unequal yoke"? (Deut. 7:2, 3; Gal.5:1; II Cor. 6:14)

20. What will be the result of not obeying God's command to withdraw from religious co-operation with false teachers? (II John 9)

6

THE WILL OF GOD FOR THE UNSAVED AND FOR THE SAVED

EVERYONE DESIRES to be a success in something. Some strive for success in business or politics, others toil for success in the entertainment world or in the arts or sports. Some even aim for success in religious fields. Now, there is nothing the matter with wanting to be a success, but there is all the difference between night and day as to the motive for success.

There is one sure way of being a success with the right goal, however, and that is to be a success with God. This is the one thing that really counts, and it not only counts for a few years of applause here on earth but for all eternity in the presence of God and the angels and all the saints in glory. "This book of the law shall not depart out of thy mouth; but thou shalt meditate therein day and night, that thou mayest observe to do according to all that is written therein: for then thou shalt make thy way prosperous, and *then thou shalt have good success*" (Josh. 1:8).

Instead of seeking earthly glory and acclaim which will fade in a short time, how much better to seek the will of God that we might have everlasting blessing! In just a few short years the names of theater stars and scientific wizards and political tycoons have drifted into the dusty past of records and libraries, and yet they gave every thought and every ounce of strength to their goal for success. How foolish it all appears in the light of eternity! "Wherefore be ye not unwise, but understanding what the will of the Lord is" (Eph. 5:17) . In other words, God is saying that if we do not seek His will, we are fools! This is what God says, so if the shoe fits, wear it!

No matter how foolish we may be, humanly speaking, or how uneducated, or how untalented in the sight of the world, we can still be a wise man and a success in the sight of God if we are sincere in seeking to know His perfect will. "If any man will do his will, he shall know" (John 7:17) . Notice, though, that it does not say, "will *know* his will" but rather, "will *do* his will." Perhaps this is the dividing point of finding the will of God or not. There are many who speak of seeking the will of God, and even Christians who say they are searching for the will of God for their lives. But they never seem to find it simply because they have no honest intention of doing God's will even if they do know it, if it does not tally with their own plans. So often we make our own plans and then submit the list to God with the demand, "Now, Lord, just sign this!"

God knows those who are really seeking to do His will, and those who are merely triflers with a superstitious, sanctimonious pretense that they are seeking His will.

I. The Will of God for Sinners

"The Lord is . . . not willing that any should perish, but that all should come to repentance" (II Peter 3:9) . This is the primary and perfect will of God for all mankind. We were created that we might glorify God and enjoy Him forever. "God our Saviour; Who will have all men to be saved, and to come unto the knowledge of the truth" (I Tim. 2:3, 4). God's heart of grace and love created man that He might pour out upon him all the blessings of the earth and the glory of Heaven, and His one desire is that men will come to Him in love for those blessings. And yet, and here is the amazing part of it all, God has given to man a free will to choose for himself whom he will serve. This truth in itself is proof that the Bible is the inspired Word of God, for it reveals a God of all power who gives to His created beings a responsible will.

The perfect will of God is for man's good. However, when man chooses his own will instead of God's will, then God lets him have his own way and reap the consequences. The permissive will of God is sometimes a terrible thing.

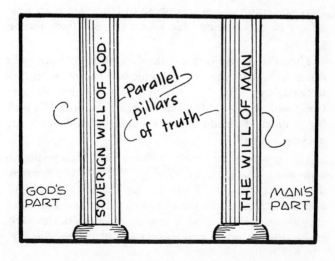

II. The Sinner's Will in Opposition to God

There are two parallel truths in doctrine: the sovereign will of God, and the responsible will of man.

Both are equally true, yet neither can be taken alone. Neither can they be reconciled nor explained. Throughout the centuries theologians have debated the two truths, one emphasizing one, and another the other. They have never been able to come to a conclusion. Those who believe only the sovereignty of God (that He wills all, plans all, and man is not a free agent) are called hyper-Calvinists. Those who stress only the will of man, that his destiny is in his own choice alone, are called Arminians.

However, the Bible-believing student of the Word of God takes the only course possible, and that is that *both doctrines are true.*

One is God's part, and His responsibility. It is well to leave the emphasis on this phase to Him. He is all powerful and all knowing. He knows the end from the beginning.

The other phase is man's responsibility. We are to be concerned with what we do with our choice, with how we exert our will. Our business is to see that we obey God's will, that we think His thoughts and seek His leading instead of thinking the thoughts of the devil and obeying his will.

This is where the whole problem lies. Man wants his own will. The same sin that was born in the heart of Satan when he said, "I will . . . be like the most High," and was carried on in the hearts of Adam and Eve when they chose their own wills instead of obedience to God, is the sin that made guilty every son of Adam who says,

"I will not!" to God. Perhaps one of the most heart-rending passages in Scripture is the cry of Christ when He says: "Ye will not come to me, that ye might have life" (John 5:40). Another is His weeping over Jerusalem when He cried: "O Jerusalem, Jerusalem . . . how often would I have gathered thy children together, even as a hen gathereth her chickens under her wings, and ye *would not!*" (Matt. 23:37). Far beyond the ken of human imagination is the truth of the King of kings and Lord of lords who allows His omnipotent hands to be tied by the puny will of rebellious man!

Instead, there is someone whom unregenerate men do choose to obey. The sinner *will do* the deeds of Satan. Jesus said to those who did not believe on Him: "Ye are of your father the devil, and the lusts of your father *ye will do*" (John 8:44).

A young man one day insisted that if he went to Hell he would glorify God. His argument was this: if it is to the glory of God to judge the sinner so that He can set up His righteous kingdom on the earth forever, then by going to Hell one is bringing about the glory of God! Just how perverted can the mind of man become? True, God will even cause the wrath of man to praise Him, but that does not mean that He *wants* man to be lost. How clear the Scripture is on this subject!

III. God's Invitation to Whosoever Will

In His love and patience, God still holds out His hands to a sinful world with the invitation, "Come!" "For God so loved the world, that he gave his only begotten Son, that whosoever believeth in him should not perish, but have everlasting life" (John 3:16). The last chapter of the Bible holds this last invitation: "And whosoever will, let him take the water of life freely" (Rev. 22:17).

If man will reject the nail-pierced hands of Christ and spend eternity in Hell will depend upon himself. He can never blame God.

The blessings of salvation are extended to all, but thrust upon none. God calls, but men must answer the call. The chosen ones are the "whosoever will" and the nonchosen ones are the "whosoever won't." There can be no election without a candidate. The foreknowledge of God permits Him to say to believers, "Chosen in him before the foundation of the world," but the invitation is given to all even as a free will is given to all.

On the last judgment day, when the lost stand before God and have been resurrected from their graves on land and in the sea, they will turn their blanched faces to the Judge, and not one will have a word to say in his own defense. They will be speechless, for they have all chosen to reject the invitation to *come* that they might have life.

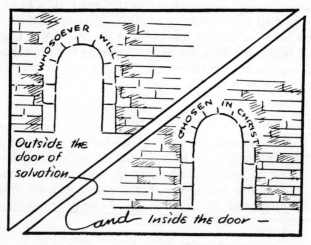

IV. Salvation Is by the Will of God

It is God who has given to man the power to think, to will, to reject. Once man has chosen to use this ability and turn to God, then the entire matter of salvation is once again in God's hands. Salvation is entirely a free gift to the willing recipient. We cannot earn it: neither is it a reward for good deeds. It is not deserved. "For by grace are ye saved through faith; and that not of yourselves: it is the gift of God: Not of works, lest any man should boast" (Eph. 2:8, 9).

Salvation is God's work in the hearts of those who accept Christ. "But as many as received him, to them gave he power to become the sons of God, even to them that believe on his name: Which were born, not of blood, nor of the will of the flesh, nor of the will of man, but of God" (John 1:12, 13). We are born into God's family by receiving God's Son as our Saviour and not by rituals or works or joining something. It is God who does the

saving: "Of his own will begat he us with the word of truth" (James 1:18).

We do not deserve to become a child of God. It is all undeserved favor that God pours out on those who will receive Him. When we are willing, God is waiting!

V. The Will of God for the Christian

This now brings us to the paramount question for those who have responded to the wooing of God, and who have placed their trust in Him. Here is where we find the margin between success and failure.

In the lifetime of our Lord here on earth, He had different circles of friends and followers, some closer and some further away, that might well illustrate what it means to be in the center of His will.

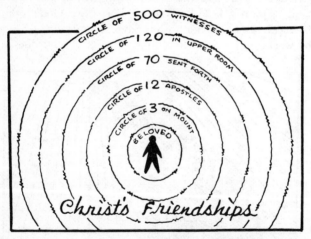

Take the first large circle of 500, who testified that they had seen Him after His resurrection. Let us call this the *outer* circle. Then came the smaller circle of 120, who **waited in the upper room in prayer and fellowship and**

experienced the Day of Pentecost. Next, we have a *still smaller* circle of 70, who were sent out to preach and heal the sick; then the *closer* circle of the 12 apostles, who were constantly with Jesus. On the Mount of Transfiguration there were the *special* 3, who beheld the glorified Christ. How the circles have closed in! But now comes the very center, the one who was closest to the heart of the Lord, the beloved apostle John. He was the one who had found the very center of the will of God. He was called the beloved disciple, no doubt because he loved the Lord most. This is the place that we should all long to occupy, the very center of the will of God, "near to the heart of God."

It is often very usual for a Christian to speak about seeking the will of God in some specific problem, event, or decision, but God is more concerned that we seek His will generally and constantly as well as for isolated needs. He would rather that we be concerned with being in harmony with Him moment by moment, and then we will indeed be led in specific decisions. The principle of living in the center of His will is the answer for any itemized problem that might arise, for the Holy Spirit will lead us step by step.

A. "Stand Perfect and Complete in All the Will of God" (Col. 4:12). No one is spiritually complete until he has found the will of God and is doing it. We know, thank God, that when we get to Heaven then we shall be sinless and perfect for we shall be "like him." But here on earth we desire to "grow in grace and in the knowledge of the Lord Jesus" and to "lack nothing" in character and deeds that would glorify Him. However much we might love babies, we have no wish that they remain babies when they are twenty years old! The same is true in the Christian life. It is surprising how many older Christians are still immature in Christ because they refuse to face this matter of the will of God in their lives in a practical way. To know God's will and reject it is to stunt our spiritual growth, for we are living in disobedience and sin. Our Lord refuses to accept any substitute for obedience. Mere lip profession or lip service is repugnant to Him. Recently a young woman said, "I think too much stress is placed on obeying God. Don't you think we should emphasize rather that we should worship and love Him?"

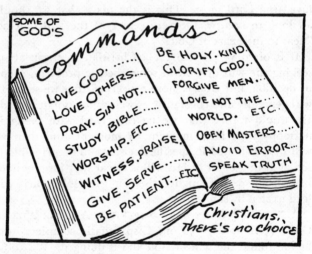

"Well, just what do worship and love involve?" I asked. "Just how do we worship Him?"

She hesitated for awhile, not knowing just what to say, so I continued, "You see, obedience is worship; obedience is love. To obey His command to attend gatherings for worship is our way of showing our love. He says, "If ye love me, keep my commandments.""

People seem to think that the contemplation of God's

will atones for disobedience; that the study of truth serves in the place of obedience. To spend much time in Bible reading and prayer, and yet refuse to attend the place of public worship is still disobedience. To attend church, but to rob God of our tithes and offerings is disobedience. To give generously, but to continue in worldliness is disobedience. The will of God is that we might be *complete* in all that He has revealed for us.

A sincerely obedient soul will not pick and choose what commands he wants to obey and what to reject. Instead he will say with Mary, the mother of Jesus: "Whatsoever he saith unto you, do it." Eyes, ears, hands, lips, body and soul—do we seriously and affectionately observe whatever Christ says to us, and do it?

Some will obey partially, but like a plow when it comes to a stone or a hard piece of earth, they balk.

B. "In Everything Give Thanks: for This Is the Will of God" (I Thess. 5:18). Godly living is a life of thanks-*living*. *In everything!* This comes as a rude shock when we think of some of the things that have come to us —sickness, poverty, disappointment and sorrow. How can we be thankful for such things? Simply because we know that God is still working all things together for good when we love Him. God has many blessings reserved for the thankful heart.

There comes to mind a certain lady who says she is a Christian, but who is such a sad soul that nothing will bring a word of cheer from her lips. She has had the average amount of earthly trouble; she has the average health and aches and pains, but to hear her talk you would think she were Job himself! No matter what kind of day it is with sunshine or snow, rain or heat, she always sighs and says, "Oh, what weather we are having!" To smile would crack her face for sure! She really enjoys her misery!

It is easy to smile and say, I'm certainly not like that! But what about our hearts in the sight of God? Are we really thankful *in everything?* It rather makes one feel a little small, does it not? How far short we come, and how often we grieve God!

C. "SUFFER ACCORDING TO THE WILL OF GOD" (I Peter 4:19). "If any man suffer as a Christian, let him not be ashamed; but let him glorify God on this behalf" (I Peter 4:16).

A poor man was literally wiped out by a flood that washed away his home and fields. But after the water had subsided, he saw something shining in the banks that the water had laid bare. It was gold. The flood that had beggared him had now made him rich!

However, the Christian has a special motive for suffering patiently, for he has the honor of suffering *for Christ.* Therefore, he should pray that he might suffer as Christ did. "Love your enemies . . . pray for them which . . . persecute you" (Matt. 5:44). "Who, when he was reviled, reviled not again; when he suffered, he threatened not" (I Peter 2:23). The Lord Jesus anticipated ahead that we should have to suffer because of our stand as Christians, and He gives no doubt as to our actions under persecution. "Blessed are they which are persecuted for righteousness' sake: for theirs is the kingdom of heaven." After all, the saints will inherit the earth some day as well as have access to Heaven, so why take it so hard when someone gossips against us now, or when old friends shun us, or someone shows discrimination against us because we are Christians? There is a special "blessed" for just such occasions. "Blessed are ye, when men shall revile you, and persecute you, and shall say all manner of evil

against you falsely, for my sake. Rejoice, and be exceeding glad: for great is your reward in heaven" (Matt. 5:
10-12).

DAILY LIVING

PERSECUTION

But we must be very sure that our persecution is because of our love for Christ and the evil spoken against
us is false. Otherwise, we deserve the trouble we bring
upon ourselves. "If ye be reproached for the name of
Christ, happy are ye" (I Peter 4:12-19; 2:19, 20).

There is a delicate line between suffering for the name
of Christ and suffering for our lack of tact. How careful
Christians must be! The world is waiting for some excuse to denounce and criticize, and they jump on the
least omission or commission with glee and say, "See,
that is what Christians do!" They all seem to know what
a Christian should be even though they are not willing to
be Christians themselves!

D. "Be Filled with the Knowledge of His Will"
(Col. 1:9). This means more than just knowing the will

of God, or even doing the will of God. Here is complete and full surrender to His will to such an extent that every room in our life is filled with His presence and approval. There is no secret closet or hidden shelf that we are keeping strictly for our besetting sin.

Very much like our homes, sometimes, we keep some special closet that is a catchall for all the things we do not know what to do with! How horrified we would be if some visitor happened to open that closet door by mistake! Is there some shelf or closet somewhere in our life that needs cleaning out? Is there some door that is kept locked against the Lord? "As the servants of Christ, doing the will of God from the heart; With good will doing service, as to the Lord" (Eph. 6:6).

E. "This Is the Will of God, even Your Sanctification" (I Thess. 4:3). Sanctification means to "be set apart for God." We are instantly set apart for God the moment we receive Christ as Saviour; set apart from the penalty of sin, from the lake of fire. This is salvation, justification, regeneration and conversion. Christians are "set-apart" ones. But every day of our Christian life we want to be more and more set apart unto God, and this is day-by-day and moment-by-moment sanctification, continuous sanctification; and this is to what the verse refers when it says that sanctification is the will of God for believers. Some day when we get to glory we shall be completely sanctified from the very presence of sin, and that will be perfect sanctification.

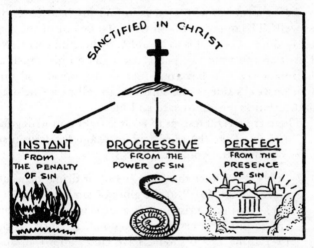

In the meantime, however, God's will is that we practice every day being set apart for God, or holy living. Just as instant sanctification saves us from the penalty of sin, and perfect sanctification saves us from the presence of sin, so continuous sanctification will deliver us from the power of sin now. It is only with the help of God that we can experience this victory over Satan and sin. "For it is God which worketh in you both to will and to do of his good pleasure" (Phil. 2:13).

Here is the climax of the whole subject, the peak of Christian desire, the epitome of success in life—sanctification. This is the answer as to what is right or wrong, or what is questionable for the Christian. "Be not conformed to this world . . . that ye may prove what is that good, and acceptable, and perfect, will of God" (Rom. 12:1, 2).

VI. The Test as to What Is Right or Wrong

To be a success with God is to find joy here on earth as well. The opposite is also true. To be out of the center of the will of God is to be unhappy here on earth. No Christian can walk two paths at the same time, much as he might try. To have one foot in the world and one foot on God's side is one sure way to fail as a Christian and to fail in joy and peace and blessing.

There are several tests as to what is right and wrong for a Christian. Take the word *joy*, for example. *J*esus first, *o*thers second, and *y*ou last.

> *J*—Jesus. "Whether therefore ye eat, or drink, or whatsoever ye do, do all to the glory of God" (I Cor. 10: 31). To put Christ first is a sure way to find joy, and to put Him first means to do all to glorify Him. Everything we do should have God's approval, and therefore His blessing. This is the first test as to what is right for a Christian. If we cannot ask God's blessing upon what we do, then we have no right to do it. *It is sin.*

the Secret of JOY and Blessing

Jesus first — (to His glory)

Others next — (that they may be saved)

You last — (a stronger Christian)

O—Others "Not seeking mine own profit, but the profit of many, that they may be saved" (I Cor. 10: 33). This is the second test as to what is right or wrong. Everything we do should be done in order that others should not be hindered from being saved. Anything that hinders others from wanting to come to Christ is wrong for a Christian. *It is sin.*

There were problems as to what was right or wrong that arose in the early Christian churches. One such problem was the matter of the meat available on the market that had been offered to idols, and was sold cheap at stalls operated by the priests from the idol temples. Those who bought the meat not only got cheaper meat, but also thought there was some benefit attached to the blessing pronounced by the priests. The question was, Should the Christians avail themselves of the cheaper meat? They knew there was no superstition attached to it as far as they were concerned, but the heathen who saw them buy from the idol's stall thought they bought the meat because they too believed in the idol.

The whole matter is summed up by: "For if any man see thee which hast knowledge sit at meat in the idol's temple, shall not the conscience of him which is weak be emboldened to eat those things which are offered to idols; And through thy knowledge shall the weak brother perish, for whom Christ died? But when ye sin so against the brethren, and wound their weak conscience, *ye sin against Christ*. Wherefore, if meat make my brother to offend, I will eat no flesh while the world standeth, lest I make my brother to offend" (I Cor. 8:4-13).

Y—You "And whatsoever ye do in word or deed, do all in the name of the Lord Jesus, giving thanks to God and the Father by him" (Col. 3:17). Everything we do should make us a stronger Christian; it should make us more thankful to God and more willing to please Him. A Christian life should be a life of thanks-*living* as well as thanks-*giving*. Anything that hinders our Christian life, or lessens our love for Christ, *is sin*.

So then, in everything we do, we should pass this three-fold test. If there is any doubt about what is right or wrong, then compare it with these Scriptures. If it cannot pass the test, it is sin for the sanctified child of God, and grieves the Spirit of God.

I know that many people rationalize, "Well, God will have to show me that this practice or habit is wrong." But just how does He show His will? Are we to wait for some voice from Heaven or a thunderbolt to jolt us into obedience? He shows us His will through His Word, and the Word of God is very clear on the principle of holiness.

A. QUESTIONABLE HABITS

For the sake of illustration, suppose we analyze the question of alcoholic drink and tobacco. Is it wrong for a Christian to drink and smoke? How often I have heard the complaint, "There is nothing in the Bible against smoking!"

But "whether therefore ye eat, or drink, or *whatsoever ye do,* do all to the glory of God" (I Cor. 10:31). Smoking is something you do! So it is included in this warning for Christians. And so is the modern dance, the theater, gambling and petting.

There are at least five reasons why a Christian should not indulge in liquor or tobacco:

1. It is harmful to the health. Everyone knows this, and there is no use denying what science proves and what the cigarette ads admit—"less nicotine . . . filters out harmful ingredients . . . less throat scratch." Why do they not come right out and say honestly, "We know

this stuff is poison, but we have doctored and toned it down so it will be slower poison than other brands"?

The Armed Forces discouraged bombadiers from smoking, for even two cigarettes were enough to cause the eyesight to be undependable and to miss the target. All the talk about lung cancer, stomach ulcers and smokers' cough must have some basis, for where there is smoke there must be fire!

There is really no need to go into detail about the harmfulness of alcoholic beverages, for all thinking persons know its harm; and if they do not, they need only take a walk down skid row to be persuaded. "But," someone complains, "I don't drink to excess. I never get drunk. I don't see anything wrong with an occasional social drink." But one drop of deadly poison is as deadly as a whole bucketful! It is not a matter of how *much* sin we do, but *any* sin.

Then comes the next argument, "But the Bible speaks

... anything that cometh of the vine ... wine or strong drink

Judges 13:14.

"WINE" REFERS TO BOTH SWEET AND FERMENTED JUICE IN SCRIPTURE

of wine as a beverage. Even Jesus turned the water into wine."

But do not forget that the word "wine" is used in Scripture to imply "beverages," and covers both fermented and unfermented drinks. "Neither let her drink *wine* or *strong drink*" (Judg. 13:14). Notice how wine here is distinguished from strong drink. "Wine" often stood simply for "drinks" or beverages, just as in China the term "drink tea" means "take refreshment."

Now comes another rationalization. "Use a little wine for thy stomach's sake" (I Tim. 5:23). It is surprising how many people must have stomach trouble! But do not forget that in the day when drugs were limited, fermented wine was used as a tonic as well as a disinfectant. This is certainly not a license for drinking it as a beverage. There are sufficient drugs today to aid digestion without drinking wine!

If there is any doubt about whether God approves fermented beverages, then listen to this: "Who hath woe? who hath sorrow? who hath contentions? who hath babblings? who hath wounds without cause? who hath redness of the eyes? They that tarry long at the wine; they that go to seek mixed wine. *Look not thou upon the wine* when it is red, when it giveth his color in the cup, when it *moveth itself aright* [bubbles in fermentation]. At the last [when fermented] it biteth like a serpent, and stingeth like an adder" (Prov. 23:29-32). Here God even forbids *looking upon* the wine, much less drinking it. The standard for an officer in the church is certainly no different from any member, and God says to them, "not given to wine" (I Tim. 3:3; Titus 1:7).

Some even try to read drunkenness into the account of the marriage at Cana (John 2). But the term, "when men have well drunk," has nothing to do with being drunk. It simply means "are satisfied," and nothing more.

Any honest seeker for the will of God surely cannot condone the beverages that have brought so much shame, degradation, poverty and heartbreak to so many homes, and have brought down so many men and women to Hell itself.

2. It is habit-forming. How true this is when someone tries to break the habit of drinking or smoking! Oh, the countless men and women I have prayed with and agonized with in their battle against these cruel masters! Christ said through the apostle Paul: "I will not be brought under the power of any" (I Cor. 6:12). "Neither yield ye your members as instruments of unrighteousness . . . but yield yourselves unto God" (Rom. 6:13).

THE SLAVE !

3. It is a stumblingblock to others. No man lives unto himself. We are all responsible for our influence. "It is good neither to eat flesh, nor to drink wine, nor anything whereby thy brother stumbleth . . . or is made weak" (Rom. 14:21) .

A young man was boasting of his zeal for God, and yet his breath reeked of tobacco. "How can you find power in witnessing for Christ when you have no victory yourself?" I asked him.

"Oh, I tell them to do as I say and not as I do!" he laughed flippantly.

"And do they do it?" I asked.

He hung his head shamefacedly, and his answer was serious. "No, I have not yet won a soul to Christ."

Praise God, he cleaned up his life and is now bringing in sheaves to the feet of his Lord!

Smoking and drinking parents lead to worldly children. Just because some Christians might smoke does not make it right. Some Christians gossip and lie too, but that does not make it right.

One father, who insisted that his smoking was nobody's business, was suddenly brought up short when his little daughter bounced into the room with a cigarette in her mouth and giggled, "See, Daddy, I'm like you!" That night I knelt with that family as that man surrendered his tobacco with tears of repentance, and he prayed, "Lord, forbid that my children will ever follow my worldliness!"

A mother argued that she saw nothing wrong in smoking. She was holding her little boy in her arms as she talked. Then the little fellow, in a gesture of happiness and love, threw his arms around her neck and bumped up against the lighted cigarette in her mouth. His smil-

ing face was bathed in tears of pain. The young mother tried to comfort him with her kisses.

"Some day your kisses won't be able to help him much when he wants to break the smoking habit," I said softly. "You will reap what you sow in your children."

"Oh, I trust he will never start the habit!" she exclaimed.

"Why not?" I asked. "If it's good enough for you, it's good enough for your boy!"

That day she confessed her sin of smoking and threw out her last package of cigarettes.

4. It is a waste of money. But you say, "It's my money, so I will do with it as I choose." If you are a child of God, your money is His too. So when you buy tobacco or liquor, you are buying it with God's money. Just where do you get money for smokes? From your family food budget, from your pleasure fund, from your tithe? Much better have a special fund and call it "funeral

fund in preparation for suicide"! If you did not smoke or drink, would you have more money for extra milk or food for the family, or money for some sick friend, for some home furniture or a church need? What a mess you make with ashes and butts and empty bottles, and alcohol rings on the furniture!

It is much better for your health and for your testimony to burn a dollar bill than to spend the dollar on doubtful habits!

A father, who was very faithful in his church and very active in religious work, still hung on to his one glass of wine each night before dinner. He warned his son about the evils of drink and told him never to touch the stuff and get the taste for it. That son grew to be a fine young fellow and very active in the church youth groups and showed great promise for the future. He even had plans to enter Bible school.

Then things began to change. He gradually dropped out of church, took up with bad companions, began to drink, and finally ended up a hopeless drunk.

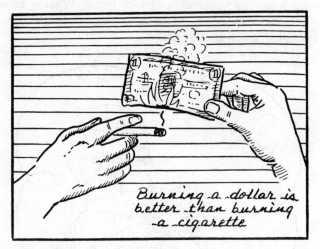

Burning a dollar is better than burning a cigarette

He was asked, "What happened, Dick? Why, you never were allowed to drink and you were always warned against liquor! How did you ever get into this state?"

With bleary eyes, and staggering gait, he slouched away with the bitter words, "But I smelled the stuff every day! It ate into my very being until I *had* to sample it for myself!"

"But you **are a Christian! How can you** go on this way?"

Dick's retort was heart-rending, "Don't preach to me! I had preaching all my life from my father, and yet he had to have his wine! I don't want to be a hypocrite like him!"

What a price to pay for one glass of wine at dinner!

5. It cannot glorify God. This is the climax of the

whole matter. This is the most important reason of all. For a Christian, this one argument should be enough to settle all questions about doubtful practices. "And whatsoever ye do in word or deed, do all in the name of the Lord Jesus, giving thanks to God and the Father by him" (Col. 3:17).

Can you imagine Christ smoking? If He would not, then we should not. "He that saith he abideth in him ought himself also so to walk, even as he walked" (I John 2:6). These are not just suggestions: these are commands.

So before lighting up a cigarette or cigar, ask yourself the following three questions: Will this glorify God? Will it help others to be Christians? Will it help my Christian life? If you can honestly answer "Yes" to these questions, then it is right. If the answer is "No," it is *sin*.

"Living in sin" does not necessarily mean some heinous social crime. It simply means that we are living in disobedience to God.

Before drinking that glass of beer or wine, ask the threefold question: Will drinking this stuff (that has been the downfall of so many) be to the glory of God? Will I be able to win others because I drink it? Will I be a better Christian because of it? If you can honestly answer "Yes," then go ahead and drink! If you cannot, then it is *sin* for you as a Christian to drink it.

After a Sunday night meeting recently, when the Lord had moved in the hearts of the people, a young man thanked me for the message. I asked if he had completely surrendered his life to the Lord. He hesitated, and then said, "Well, I am a chain smoker and I'm afraid to promise God that I will stop smoking in case I might fail."

"Why not confess your failure, and let Christ take over your life and give you victory?" I asked.

The tears came to his eyes. "How I wish I could!"

"Then why not do it right now?" I asked.

"Wait a minute, and I will call my father," the young man said. "He is a deacon in the church and he smokes as much as I do!"

Soon the family gathered in the corner of the church. The godly mother was in much prayer. I found that the son's fiancée was unsaved. So the next hour was spent in leading her to the Lord, in dealing with the father and son, and seeing them surrender their lives and habits to the Lord. As they left the church that night, their faces were wet with tears but with smiles of joy and hope of victory.

Implanted within us is a desire for amusement and enjoyment. Christianity is only against that which is hurtful to the Christian testimony.

The following article is quoted from a Christian magazine:

How to Use Tobacco

Some time ago, a tobacco company sent packages of cigarettes to some high school boys, with this explanation, "We are sending you a package of our finest cigarettes. We hope you will use them to your satisfaction and want some more.

One of the boys used the cigarettes and wrote back, "I received your package of cigarettes, and used them to my satisfaction. I steeped them in a quart of water, and sprayed our bug-infested rose bushes. Every bug died. The cigarettes are sure a good poison. I want some more next year if any bugs survive!"

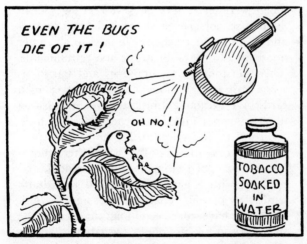

This young fellow knew how to use tobacco! He had sense enough to use it to poison bugs instead of himself!

Take the matter of card playing, for instance. Again I quote from an article:

How can any who profess to love the Lord waste their time, to say the least, by engaging in a game so unquestionably high on the list of the Devil's tools, is hard to understand. Anyone who plays cards for a prize is a gambler, and gambling is legalized robbery.

Read the following story taken from another Christian magazine, and let it be a warning to any who might think it entertaining or smart to play cards:

Just before a meeting one morning, a tramp dropped into the church and made his way to a certain pew. "Our family used to sit in this pew," he said. "It is the first church I ever attended. My father was an officer in this church. There were seven of us boys who sat together in Sunday school class and we had great respect and love for our teacher. We used to go to her house on Saturdays for music and refreshments. Then she thought to amuse us and taught us some card tricks. None of us had ever used cards. We became enthusiastic over it, learning different games, and our teacher played with us. Soon we stopped going to her house and spent our spare time playing cards with other fellows. Then we stopped going to Sunday school, and took up with a gang who smoked and drank while they played. That was years ago. Two of those boys have since been hung; three are in the state's prison for life; one is a vagabond like myself. All I wish is that that Sunday school teacher had not taught us to play cards."

As the man stood there brokenhearted, an elderly woman, who was sitting near the pulpit, rose and went closer to him. Then with a scream of, "Oh, God! I am that Sunday school teacher!" she fell to the floor in a faint.

When you gamble. you are stealing from others if you win, and stealing from your family and God if you lose. Either way, it is wrong.

B. Questionable Amusements

What about the modern dance? Once again I quote, "The real pleasure in dancing, whether one is aware of it or not, is emotional stimulus. There are those who will say, 'I dance for the music,' or 'I dance for the exercise,' but these are not the real reasons. You can enjoy music in other ways, and there are many other ways to get exercise. The modern dance breaks down moral inhibitions. Liberties are taken on the dance floor that would not be allowed elsewhere. If you were to come home one evening and find some man embracing your wife, what would you do? Perhaps you would give him a piece of your fist as well as a piece of your mind! And rightly so! And yet, on the dance floor anyone can embrace anyone else, and it is all supposed to be purely platonic.

Dancing tends to make a girl secondhand on the marriage bargain counter. No high-minded young man wants a girl who has been embraced and kissed by dozens of other men. If she is loose before marriage she will likely be afterward.

Dancing has caused many divorces. Homes are broken up because of dancing with other people's husbands and wives. Lust is aroused.

I was talking to a young convert about his craze for dancing, and he asked me, "Is it all right for me to dance?" I answered, "Yes!" He was amazed and repeated his question, thinking I had not heard aright. "Yes," I said, "you can dance all you want to with your own wife in your own home!"

"Oh," he was disappointed, "that's no fun!"

That about hits the nail on the head, does it not? The main attraction about the modern dance is the attraction between boy and girl.

Now we come to another question. What is wrong with the theater?

The institution of the theater is sponsored by godless men and women, and has always stood for immorality and shady reputation. The films presented are a feeder of lust, a perverter of morals, a school of crime. They glorify impurity as love; picture murder as entertainment; exalt nakedness as beauty; show drinking, divorce, reveling, gambling and gun fights as proper and legitimate. They ruin the influence of the Christian; debauch the minds of children; inflame the lusts of youth; harden the hearts of sinners. Recent studies show that in America 77 million people attend the movies once a week, and only 19 million attend Sunday school.

But someone comes back with the excuse, "But I only attend the good films!" But just what about the Hollywood religious films? They are put out by atheists and unsaved producers, writers and actors. Just what sort of religious influence do they have? Many people are getting their religion from such Hollywood films, and so they have the same wrong teachings that are formulated by the world, "Do good, be good, and all will be well!" Even so-called Bible subject films are so filled with imagination and fabrication, sensuality and lust, that they are anything but true to Bible principles. I have had people argue with me on some Bible incident, and used for their proof, "Why, I saw it in the movies!" Whenever there might be a "good" film shown in a theater, they usually have a second feature of something "spicy" to appeal to those who might not buy a ticket for a good film. Remember, Christian, when you look at a film, God is watching it with you!

To summarize it all, if you can honestly ask God to bless you as you go to the dance, or the movies, or to play cards, and if you know that you are glorifying Him by going, and that you can witness to your partner or companions, and that you will be more encouraged to attend prayer meeting because you do these things, then go ahead! If you cannot pass the threefold test, then *it is sin*.

Now, go back to that passage in Romans 12:1, 2, take it phrase by phrase and see just what God is saying to Christians.

"I beseech you therefore, brethren." Just imagine! Here the Almighty God is begging us to seek His will!

Although He made us: "For of him, and through him, and to him, are all things: to whom be glory forever. Amen" (Rom. 11:36), yet He beseeches us to yield our wills to Him *for our good!* Oh, the indescribable grace of God!

"By the mercies of God." Because of His mercy and love and grace; and because He made us and because He wants to bless us; and because He saved us from Hell, and—well, after all, just how many more reasons do we need?

"That ye present your bodies a living sacrifice." Christ may not ask all of us to lay down our lives for Him as martyrs, but He does ask us to live for Him. To be sure, it might sometimes seem easier to die a glorious martyr's death and be on the front pages of the newspapers than to live a humdrum day-by-day life of consistent holy living. A sacrifice is "something given over to the use of another." We do not lose it, but rather God will use it to much better advantage. In other words, we are asked to give back to the use of God the body and soul that belong to Him in the first place, and which He has loaned us for the short years we live here on the earth. How unbelievable it is when some sin-blinded soul rejects this plea of God and refuses to give back to His heavenly Father the life that was only loaned him in the first place!

"Holy, acceptable unto God." The only gift that is acceptable to God is a holy sacrifice. In Old Testament days, all the sacrifices of animals had to be in perfect health and beauty. It was always the firstfruits of the land that were acceptable to God, and not the leftover dregs. So with us today, our service, our time, our talents, our very life must be holy if it is to be acceptable. "As obedient children . . . be ye holy in all manner of conversation [living]; Because it is written, Be ye holy; for I am holy" (I Peter 1:14-16).

"Which is your reasonable service." It is just plain common sense that we owe all we are and have to Him who gave us richly all things to enjoy. This is our intelligent service. We are not asked to serve God in blind superstition and ritual, but because we are informed as to His person and His work and His holiness, we are told precisely how to live for Him. He does not leave us struggling in doubt.

"And be not conformed to this world." Do not be poured into the same mold as the world. Even Christians today seem afraid to be different from the world. They follow the smutty language, the suggestive dress, the Hollywood makeup, just as if they actually approved it all. God does not ask us to be quaint or strange, but we certainly do not have to be worldly just to keep up with the crowd.

It was during the last World War when our family were prisoners of the Japanese in Manila, that our small boys found themselves without many toys. They did have a lead soldier, but you can't have much fun with one lone soldier! But they solved the problem by making more soldiers from bits of lead that they dug up from the ground around our bamboo hut. The ground was reclaimed land, and had been filled in with junk and fill over a space of many years, and when trying to plant a few vegetables to stay off the pangs of hunger one would dig up inner tubes, pots and pans, etc., and lead pipe.

Our youngsters wetted down the mud floor of the hut, carefully pressed their one lone soldier into the soft clay and withdrew him, and then poured in melted lead. When the lead was hard, behold, a new soldier was made!

They were able to build quite an army in this way, and trade them off to playmates for other toys.

But one day I was watching as the younger son tried to imitate his older brother and make his own soldiers. He gingerly pressed the soldier into the clay. But when he turned to get the melted lead his foot kicked a small stone into the mold. I paid little attention until the mold was broken away and the new soldier held up for inspection. Then came the wail, "Mom, my soldier has no head!" The stone had blocked the mold and the soldier was made without a head!

God so loves His Son that He wants us all to be "conformed to the image of his Son" (Rom. 8:29). Literally, to be poured into the same mold. "For even Christ pleased not himself" (Rom. 15:3). But instead of being in the image of Christ, too often we are found in the image of the world. Just which mold are we using? Or are we so rebellious and wayward that stones of sin have slipped into the mold, and God's "soldiers have no heads"?

"But be ye transformed by the renewing of your mind." A new mind is the gift of God, even as a new life and a new name and a new home are all part of salvation. Transformed and transfigured! The result will show in new habits, new ambitions, new friends, new appetites and a new appearance as well.

Now, and only now, it is that we can prove the full blessing of God.

"That ye may prove what is that good, and acceptable, and perfect, will of God." Here, and only here, is the center of His will, the place of good success. Here is the place of rest and peace and blessing that every heart craves.

Are we willing? God is waiting! Why not surrender

to Him right now, and ask Him to take over completely and pour us into the image of His Son?

VII. The Result of Not Doing the Will of God

This is addressed to Christians. Does it matter if I obey God or not? As long as I am saved and going to Heaven, does it matter if I glorify Him here on earth? Well, such questions bespeak great ignorance of the Word of God, or great coldness of heart. You might ask, Does it matter if I love my husband or not? Does it matter if I make him happy or sad? I'm married anyway, so why keep up the effort of loving and pleasing him? Well, the analogy fails in this respect, for the husband might leave you and love another. God never will! But the very question shows coldness of heart and rejection of the marriage vows. Something is radically wrong!

When we fail to seek the will of God, not only are we fools but we are also grieving Him. We become a stumblingblock to others; we lose our reward in Heaven; we bring trouble and sorrow upon ourselves right here on earth.

"And that servant, which knew his lord's will, and prepared not himself, neither did according to his will, shall be beaten with many stripes" (Luke 12:47). No, we do not get away with anything. We will always reap what we sow, and God will always discipline His wayward child.

How much better to pray even as our Lord Jesus, "Nevertheless not my will, but thine be done!"

"He that doeth the will of God abideth forever" (I John 2:17).

YIELD YOUR BODY*

Daniel 3:28

Would you have a faith that sings?
  Yield your body!
Would you change the word of kings?
  Yield your body!
Would you pass through sufferings
With the joy Christ's presence brings,
So no smell of burning clings?
  Yield your body!

Romans 12:1, 2

Would you serve your God with skill?
  Yield your body!
Would you conquer this world's ill?
  Yield your body!
Would you have the Spirit fill
And renew your mind, until
You can prove God's perfect will?
  Yield your body!

I Corinthians 9:24-27

Would you glorify God's Son?
  Yield your body!
Would you see poor sinners won?
  Yield your body!
Are you longing so to run,
In the race that you've begun,
That your Lord may say, "Well done"?
  Yield your body!

—T. M. Sellers

°Written after hearing a message by Mr. Friederichsen, on some of our experiences during the last World War while interned in the Philippines.

QUESTIONS

1. What is the secret of success with God? (Josh. 1:8)
2. Who is a fool? (Eph. 5:17)
3. How can we know the will of God? (John 7:17)
4. What is God's perfect will for the lost? (II Peter 3:9; I Tim. 2:3, 4)
5. Why are sinners lost? (John 5:40; Matt. 23:37)
6. Who may be saved? (Rev. 22:17)
7. Can anyone be saved by works or good deeds? (Eph. 2:8, 9)
8. By whose will are men born again? (John 1:12; James 1:18)
9. What is God's will for the Christian? (Col. 4:12; I Thess. 5:18; I Peter 4:19; Col. 1:9; I Thess. 4:3)
10. How should we do the will of God? (Eph. 6:6)
11. What is the test of what is right or wrong for a Christian? (I Cor. 10:31-33; Col. 3:17)
12. When we cause others to stumble, against whom are we sinning? (I Cor. 8:4-13)

13. Should a Christian indulge in any habit-forming practice? (I Cor. 6:12)
14. What does God beg of us Christians? (Rom. 12:1, 2)
15. How can we yield our bodies? (Dan. 3:28; I Cor. 9:24-27; Rom. 6:13)
16. Does God approve the use of alcoholic beverages? (Prov. 23:29-32; I Tim. 3:3; Titus 1:7)
17. Does "wine" in the Bible always mean alcoholic drink? (Judg. 13:14)
18. What should be our motive in service for God? (Eph. 6:6)
19. What brings a reward in Heaven? (Matt. 5:10-12)
20. What attitude should a Christian take toward those who oppose the Gospel? (Matt. 5:44)

7

THE WILL OF GOD IN
TEMPTATION

THERE ARE TWO MEANINGS in Scripture for the word "temptation"; one means "to try, to test, to determine worth," and the other "to solicit to do evil."

In this chapter we are dealing with the second meaning, the temptation to do evil. Satan tempts us to develop our wickedness; but God tries us to develop our faith. There is nothing nobler than to resist temptation to evil. "He that ruleth his spirit" is greater "than he that taketh a city" (Prov. 16:32). Sin consists, not in being tempted, but in yielding to temptation.

A minister was once asked by a friend, "How many members do you have in your church?"

"One thousand," the preacher replied.

"Really!" his friend was impressed. "And how many are active members?"

"All of them are active," came the unexpected reply; "about two hundred of them are active for the Lord, the balance are active for the Devil!"

Remember, our life as a Christian is active either for the Lord or for the Devil. Many professing Christians think because they are not doing anything especially wicked that they are living for God. The fact is, a re-

ACTIVE FOR GOD

IN MANY CHURCHES IT'S EIGHT TO TWO

ACTIVE FOR SELF

spectable life may not be enlisted in active and positive service for God. Therefore, not to be helping the cause of God according to one's ability simply means that the life might be hindering the work of God. That is what the Devil is doing too.

I. Who Is the Tempter?

The archenemy of the child of God is the enemy of God Himself, the Devil. True, the idea of a personal Devil has long since gone out of style with the world, and has even become a ridicule instead of a fear. But that is because men have read their own fancies into the Scriptures instead of taking the Word of God alone. They have read *Paradise Lost* instead of the Book of Job. They have taken men's dreams and wild imaginations instead of the facts of truth. The very image of a being with horns, a tail and a pitchfork has been conjured up by the Devil himself so as to cause men to laugh instead of quake, to deny his very existence so he can further his wicked cause.

An elderly Christian was looking at a picture of Satan with the traditional horns and ugly face, and he said, "If Satan came to me looking like that I think I would give him a good fight! But instead he comes to me in the form of a nice comfortable nap on Sunday mornings instead of going to church!"

To deny the person of the Devil, some simply drop the "*D*" and call him "evil." But God says that this great enemy is a person, and not just an influence. There can be no influence without personality. The personal pronoun *he* is used when speaking of Satan, and the characteristics of personality are attributed to him. He walks, speaks, thinks, rules, and is called the "prince of the power of the air," the "god of this world." His other names are Lucifer, Beelzebub, Satan, the wicked one (Eph. 2:2; John 12:31; 13:2; Matt. 13:19, 39; II Cor. 4:4), for he is the agent of evil and not just evil itself.

A minister was recently visiting new converts, who had accepted Christ through my Bible class, and was trying to get them to return to his church. They had changed from his very liberal church to attending a Bible-preaching church, and were trying to tell him why. They asked him about his beliefs on the doctrines of the Bible. When they came to the subject of Hell and the Devil the minister laughed outright and scorned them for being medieval!

His attitude did more to persuade them against returning to his church than all the talking I might have done.

Ridicule will not eliminate the Devil. He is the king over his own realm of demons and fallen angels, the kingdom of darkness (Luke 11:14-18). His one desire is to keep men from God (II Cor. 4:4), and to spoil the fellowship of those who belong to God (I Tim. 3:7; I Peter 5:8, 9).

With all his power, however, Satan is still subservient to God, for his power and knowledge are limited and he can only do that which God will allow (Job 1). Although he is the author of sin and the epitome of all that is against good, yet Satan must be subject to God and he hates every moment of it.

The Devil is not omnipresent (everywhere), so he uses his emissaries, the demons, to do his dastardly work of tempting (Matt. 12:43-45). Because he is not omniscient (all knowing), he does not know our thoughts even though he tries to influence our minds (Acts 5:3). Although Satan is not omnipotent (all powerful), he is stronger than mankind, and can do more than all of us put together. How much we need the help of God to overcome him (James 4:7)!

The one and only thing that Satan has created is *sin* (Ezek. 28:13-15; Isa. 14:12-15). When he came up against the Son of God, however, he was vanquished (Matt. 4:1-10).

This, then, is the enemy we face as children of God. He does not have to concern himself too much with those who are dead in trespasses and sins; he lets them drift along in his trail, but he has active interest in the wide-awake Christian. The Devil does not bother with spiritual cemeteries; he has no interest in the spiritually dead.

This chapter is particularly concerned with the Christian and his connection with temptation.

Christ hath "delivered us from the power of darkness, and hath translated us into the kingdom of his dear Son"

(Col. 1:13). We now become the special targets of the fiery darts of the Evil One as he seeks revenge for our having escaped his fate in the lake of fire. The word "Devil" means "slanderer or accuser," and, oh, how Satan works overtime to spoil the fellowship of a Christian with his heavenly Father! It is well to be informed against him, and be prepared for his onslaughts.

II. The Result of Yielding to Temptation

"But every man is tempted, when he is drawn away of his own lust, and enticed. Then when lust hath conceived, it bringeth forth sin: and sin, when it is finished, bringeth forth death" (James 1:14, 15). The word "death" means "separation."

When Satan sinned he was cast out from God's presence where he had been the leader of the worship and destroyed the creation of God on the earth so that it became without form and void for billions of years. Then when God created man, Satan again entered the remade world and ruined the perfect creation by tempting man and causing him to fall from his original fellowship with God.

Ever since, the sin of Adam and Eve, like a ghastly illness, has been passed on down to every descendant of the human race, so that all men are born with a sinful nature. We are double sinners: sinners by nature (Ps. 51:5), and sinners by choice and practice (Rom. 3:23).

The result of Satan's choice, "*I will* be like the most High," caused him to fall from Heaven. The result of Adam's and Eve's sin, "*I will* take the forbidden fruit," caused them to lose fellowship with God and to reap the curse of God not only upon themselves, but also upon all nature and all future human beings. The result of our sin, "*I will* have my own way instead of God's way," will cause the wrath of God to fall on us *unless* we take God's way of salvation.

The wrath of God is *death:* physical death, spiritual death and eternal death.

But notice how in each case sin took the same form, *"I will* have my own way!" It is self-will against God's will.

It is interesting to note how often, when the Bible gives a list of sins that are repulsive to God or that bring judgment upon men, the list may include some so-called big sins, some moderate sins, *and* the little sins too! God puts them all together in one list and names them all *sin.*

So, self-will is the essence of sin. From this one evil source come pride, jealousy, bitterness, evilspeaking, self-pity, anger, laziness, etc. These are the more prevalent sins of the Christian.

Before we receive Christ as our personal Saviour we have the one evil nature called in Scripture by such names as "the old man" or "the natural man." We are controlled by Satan; we are his child (John 8:44). Our life is governed by the soul—the selfish desires, and we are dead in sins (Eph. 2:2, 3). There is not too much problem concerning how to live, for we want our own way and take our own way, and the only conflict we have is with other people who also want their own way.

OUR OLD NATURE IS SATAN—CONTROLLED

SATAN

But when we are born again, we are given a new nature which is born of God and is called "the new man" or "the spiritual man" created in Christ Jesus. This new nature does not love sin, and desires the will of God instead of self-will. Now the battle begins! These two natures are opposites and at variance with each other, and we find ourselves crying out with the apostle Paul: "For that which I do I allow [approve] not: for what I would, that do I not; but what I hate, that do I . . . For the good that I would I do not: but the evil which I would not, that I do" (Rom. 7:15, 19).

The Devil does not often tempt a Christian to murder or drunkenness. Instead he trips us into self-seeking or envy or discontent. They are just as much sin as any other evil deed, and just as much sin as not to obey God. "Therefore to him that knoweth to do good, and doeth it not, to him it is sin" (James 4:17).

III. How Does Temptation Come to the Christian?

One way to catch a horse is to approach him with an apple held out in one hand and a halter hidden behind the back in the other hand. Satan uses the same tactics. He holds out to us a tempting morsel, and then when we yield to it he throws the halter over our head and leads us into sin. He spreads out an enticing bait of money, a sweet smile, fragrant wine, self-glory, and then throws the net over our head while we are stopping to investigate.

A. TEMPTATION COMES THROUGH THE NATURAL DESIRES OF THE FLESH

We make ourselves available for temptation because of our human and physical natures. It is the natural man that lusts for the forbidden fruit of self-will against God's will, and we are tempted because we are open to temptation. "Every man is tempted, when he is drawn away of his own lust, and enticed" (James 1:14).

When we hearken to the voice of the tempter, we are enticed; when we obey his voice, we sin; when we sin, we lose our fellowship with God (James 1:15). For the lost sinner the wages of sin is eternal death, but for the child of God the wages of sin is lost fellowship. Thank God, He has promised us everlasting life and that we shall never perish (John 10:27, 28)!

But Satan uses the same means on us as he used in the Garden of Eden—"the lust of the flesh, and the lust of the eyes, and the pride of life" (I John 2:16).

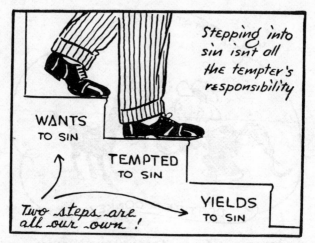

First of all though, Eve was definitely available for temptation for she must have been in the vicinity of the forbidden tree. She was not content with all the trees in the garden, but thought that she was being robbed of this one delicacy and that God was holding out something, and so she was good material for the Devil. He is still looking for those who are available for his devices, and any excuse is good enough for him to try to whisper evil thoughts and suggestions into our ears. Discouragement, weariness, physical weakness, idle curiosity, secret lust, discontent, it matters not what the condition, they all bespeak lack of faith and trust in our Lord and a lack of love for His Word, His work, or His people.

This is the opportunity Satan is seeking.

In the Garden of Eden, Satan appeared in the form of a serpent, the cleverest and most attractive of all the created animals, and to make it even more unusual, he causes the beast to speak. Can we wonder that Eve was intrigued?

AVAILABLE FOR TEMPTATION

His first question was, "Hath God said . . .?" How familiar this sounds! We hear it on every side from the skeptics, the modernists, the cults and errors. Doubts! The everlasting question mark, the Devil's own wedge.

Then it is that Eve makes her next mistake for she listens to the words of doubt and talks back. But Eve was not content to talk back in rebuke to the tempter. She chattered on and changed the Word of God (Gen. 3:1-6), and then even added to it of her own invention. Here again is the method of the modern errors. Men change the words of God and add to them and take away from them to suit themselves. Even good Christians sometimes exclaim, "Why, what is wrong with that religion? They use the Bible. They have verses to back what they teach!" And yet if men would investigate they would find that some are to a great extent false doctrine and inventions of man, with just a few verses from the Bible to try to prove what they say. And if honestly examined, they would also find that those verses do not really fit in with the subject at all. They were simply wresting the Scriptures. Stick to the Word! Only the Word and *all* the Word!

1. The lust of the eyes. Eve *saw* that the fruit was pleasant to the *eyes*. So much temptation comes through to the mind by means of the eyes. Licentious pictures, lustful books, godless entertainment, unholy sights, all appeal to the sensual appetite in the unconsecrated Christian, and it is sad to see how the invitation to sin is spreading into Christian homes through uncontrolled television and magazines. Unrest and dissatisfaction are

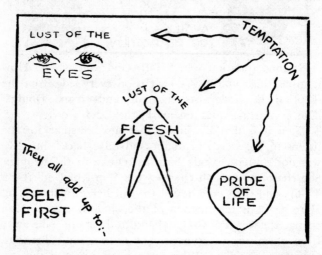

generated by the Hollywood standards of glamor and love, until a husband begins to think he is not happily married unless his wife is a creamy-skinned Miss America; and the wife feels she is being robbed of love because her husband is not tall, dark and handsome and constantly whispering sweet compliments into her ear and worshiping at her feet! In Sunday school, the little children sing the song, "Be careful, little eyes, what you see." Well be careful, grown-up eyes, what you see and read!

2. The lust of the flesh. Eve saw that the fruit was good for *food*. Her appetite was aroused. Satan appeals to our appetites too, and nothing gives him more satisfaction than to see a Christian bound by the lust of the flesh. Gluttony, immorality, doubtful habits, self-pampering and mere satisfaction of the physical senses all lead to the desire to enjoy that which is contrary to the will and glory of God. God gave us our five senses, but He expects us to use godliness as a guide to what is right or wrong. The great lust for comfort is a weakness of elderly people, and they sometimes are willing to forget the will of God just to be comfortable. The lust for experience is typical of youth, but God wants the Christian to use *sense* in the use of his senses!

3. The pride of life. Eve saw that the forbidden fruit was desired to make one wise. There is nothing wrong with being wise, but choosing worldly wisdom contrary to the will of God is certainly not wisdom at all. In each of us is the inherent urge to be something, to keep up with "the Joneses," to possess more than others, to be more important than others, to know more than others. It all simmers down to *pride*. Ambition becomes wrong when we listen to the voice of Satan to accomplish it. To gain prestige, power or wealth by disobeying the will of God is very far short of being wise. "Professing themselves to be wise, they became fools" (Rom. 1:22). The wisdom of this world might puff us up in the sight of men, but when we go against the will of God we are yielding to the will of the Devil. This craving of self, the ego, is the main chink through which Satan can shoot home his fiery darts.

But Eve did not stop with just being tempted. The

next step was that she *took* of the forbidden fruit. Now sin is born in the heart of the human race. And sin loves company just as misery loves company. No one likes to backslide alone; it is too uncomfortable to be the only one out of step, so the sinner tries to drag someone else down with him. Eve gives the fruit to Adam.

Throughout history, Eve has borne the main blame for the first sin, and the curse upon womanhood has been weakness and sorrow and pain, as well as to be subject to her husband. But for womanhood, as well as for man, there is a remedy from that curse in the coming of the Christ, *the Child,* the Saviour of the world. "Nevertheless she shall be saved in the bearing of the child" (I Tim. 2:13-15, literal).

B. TEMPTATION COMES THROUGH NEGLECT OF THE
   WORD OF GOD, and unbelief in the truth of God.

By using false teachers and ministers, Satan appears as an angel of light to confuse and distract the seeker after truth (II Cor. 11:14, 15). Not only do wrong religions and Modernism twist and add to the Scriptures, they even deny God's Word. Just like the serpent came right out and said, "Ye shall not surely die" (Gen. 3:4), so many false teachings say, "There is no Hell, etc., etc."

True enough, Adam and Eve did not fall down and die right then and there. But the word "death" means "separation," and there are three kinds of death spoken of in the Bible. Physical death is when the person leaves the body; spiritual death is when the sinner is separated from God, even though he is physically alive; eternal death is everlasting separation from God in the lake of fire.

The moment Adam and Eve sinned, they were separated from God's fellowship and were spiritually dead in trespasses and sins. Later on, they did die physically. They would have died eternally as well, except for the covering that God provided when the blood of some animal was shed as a type of the blood of Christ, which is the remedy for guilty sinners. So the Devil lied after all! Those who follow his lies today and deny God's revealed truth about Hell will some day find themselves in the very Hell they deny.

The Forked Road

VICTORY

TEMPTATION

DEFEAT

IV. How to Overcome the Tempter

There is really no excuse for any Christian to yield to the Devil. When we accept Christ as our personal Saviour, He is not only able to save us from Hell, but is able to save us from the power of Satan as well. "Greater is he [Christ] that is in you, than he [Satan] that is in the world" (I John 4:4). "The Son of God was manifested, that he might destroy the works of the devil" (I John 3:8). With Almighty God in us and with us, surely victory is available *if we want it.*

No man ever entered a "blind alley" of temptation. The road is always a forked road, and one fork leads out of the difficulty. We may say that we desire victory, but secretly we do not. Instead, we enjoy our sin and hope to continue just as long as we can get away with it. It is possible for a Christian to deplore his lack of victory over his temper, but the truth of the matter is that he enjoys "blowing his top" and watching his family scamper from his tantrums!

A. VICTORY IS AVAILABLE BY FAITH IN A VICTORIOUS LORD

"This is the victory that overcometh the world, even our faith" (I John 5:4). Faith is to believe God's Word that He will do what He says. He says He will give victory, so why not claim it?

God is on our side! The victorious life is a normal life.

"Oh," someone says, "but I am human, and it's human to sin!" It certainly is human to sin, but when we have been born from above we are a child of the King! He that is born of God does not practice sin (I John 3:9). The child of God is *extraordinary!* We are ordinary, the Holy Spirit indwelling us is the *extra*. Combine the two and you have *extraordinary!* When the Holy Spirit and the Christian work together in harmony, the extraordinary will be accomplished.

An Eastern legend tells of a king who was ill. He sent a servant to bring a bowl of precious medicine from the apothecary across town. The street was busy and a fair was in full swing with all its attractions and crowds, so the servant had difficulty in bringing the bowl of liquid safely. However, he did so without spilling one drop.

The king asked him, "How is it that you could bring

the potion so quickly without spilling any when the streets were so crowded?"

The answer was simple, "I was thinking only of the medicine. I noticed nothing but the bowl in my hands."

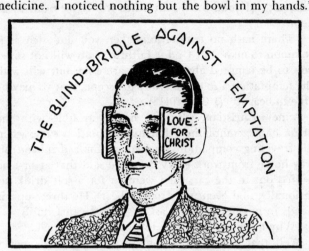

This is also the secret of avoiding temptation. Fix our minds on the Lord, and we will not be tempted to sin. Victory is moment by moment and step by step. Cease *trying* to be good, and let God help you to be good. Live in the present with God. Claim victory *right now*. Each time temptation comes, call upon Him and say, "Lord, You take over. Keep me!"

"Now thanks be unto God, which always causeth us to triumph in Christ" (II Cor. 2:14).

B. Co-operate with God

"Neither give place to the devil" (Eph. 4:27). Do not give him standing room. If we do not want to buy his wares, we had better flee from the Devil's shop. "Resist the devil, and he will flee from you" (James 4:7). Sometimes we can answer our own prayers by keeping ourselves out of the way of temptation. "He that is begotten of God keepeth himself, and that wicked one toucheth him not" (I John 5:18). In other words, *we want to be kept.*

"There hath no temptation taken you but such as is common to man: but God is faithful, who will not suffer you to be tempted above that ye are able; but will with the temptation also make a way to escape, that ye may be able to bear it" (I Cor. 10:13).

A new Christian, who was having trouble with the drink habit, complained that his temptation came when his traveling companion stopped off for a drink on his way home from work every day. He said that at first he waited out in the car, then went in for a soft drink occasionally, and eventually took a beer. He threw up his hands in hopelessness and asked, "What can I do?"

"Why not find a new ride to work?" I suggested.

Well, that was all there was to it. He got a new means of transportation, and the problem was solved.

Avoiding temptation is easier than trying to overcome it. We can "keep ourselves" by avoiding the sights and sounds and smells and friends of the world. "Little children, keep yourselves from idols" (I John 5:21). "Let everyone that nameth the name of Christ depart from iniquity" (II Tim. 2:19).

God could work a private miracle and take us by the ear and remove us out of the way of temptation, but He does not. He gives us the credit to have enough desire and sense to want to co-operate with Him. Too often we try to get as close to sin as we dare, and then wonder why we do not lose our appetite for it.

A good formula for victory is found in Psalm 1:1, 2: "Blessed is the man that *walketh* not in the counsel of

the ungodly, nor *standeth* in the way of sinners, nor *sitteth in* the seat of the scornful. But his delight is in the law of the Lord; and in his law doth he meditate day and night." The word "blessed" means "congratulations." God congratulates the man who keeps out of the way of temptation and meditates in the Word of God day and night. Satan does not have much of a chance with such protection as that!

A lad, who had been converted from a life of worldliness, was so enthusiastic in his new faith and Bible study, that he was a joy to all who loved the Lord. He used to be an exhibitionist dancer and had been in great demand as an entertainer. It was a real test when he had to refuse many calls to perform.

But one night he failed the Lord, and took part in the dancing in the public market. I was disappointed when I heard of it, but I waited for him to tell me about it. "David, why did you go back to dancing when you had given it up?" I asked him.

"Well," he hesitated, "you see, I had no intention of dancing. I just went to watch the others. Then a girl I used to dance with begged me to dance, and, well, I found myself back in the old routine."

"David," I told him, "you can see that your trouble was that you didn't stay away from the place of temptation. You first walked over to the place where they were dancing, then you stood to watch, and so you settled down in sin. Next time, better keep away entirely!"

C. WATCH AND PRAY

"Watch and pray, that ye enter not into temptation" (Matt. 26:41).

Prayer is the power of the church and the ammunition of the Christian warrior. We need to stand on guard against the Devil and be as alarmed at the entrance of an evil thought as if it were the hiss of a serpent. Prayer is not intended to encourage indolence. When we pray for deliverance from sin, we should also watch and fight against it. To pray for victory and still hold on to some known sin is hypocrisy. It is just as foolish to pray for physical health and then drink poison! We are fooling no one but ourselves. Whatever we find to be the enemy of the work of God in our souls we must be ready to sacrifice, though it might be as dear to us as our right hand.

It is when men allow Satan to bind them that they make the foolish bargain to prefer their own will to Christ's, and sin to holiness. Had Satan tried to tempt Peter when he was on the Mount of Transfiguration, he would have tempted in vain; but when he found Peter in wrong company, he succeeded.

A young Christian who had such a glowing testimony and whose very face shone with love for the Lord was a constant joy to my heart. I was gone from town for some time, and then when I returned, I could hardly believe my eyes when I saw her again. How she had changed! Gone were the smile and the glow; in fact, she even tried to avoid meeting me. What happened?

Instead of giving up her old worldly friends, she had kept up with the excuse that she was going to win them to Christ. Instead, she had dropped back into their worldly ways and lost her testimony. She neglected her time of prayer and Bible reading; she dropped out of the Bible classes; she stopped going to church. Oh, how the Lord had to discipline that girl before she came back into full surrender to Him!

Prayer will keep us from sin, and sin will keep us from prayer. Satan trembles when he sees a Christian on his knees; he is a coward and will run at the drop of a hat.

D. PUT ON THE WHOLE ARMOR OF GOD

"Put on the whole armor of God, that ye may be able to stand against the wiles of the devil" (Eph. 6:11-18).

God has given us protection against the enemy. Our part is to keep it buckled on. Each piece of this spiritual armor is a practical therapy against sin.

The belt of truth. Truth in belief, truth in practice, truth in word and deed are all weapons against temptation. How easy it is sometimes for Christians to be a little shady in business, or off center in truth, and how much harm they do to the cause of Christ! God requires truth in the heart, through and through.

The breastplate of righteousness. This protects our heart as we strive for holiness day by day. To keep righteous before God is to keep in fellowship with Him. "If we walk in the light, as he is in the light, we have fellowship one with another, and the blood of Jesus **Christ** his Son cleanseth us from all sin" (I John 1:7).

The shoes of peace. Our feet are protected from the thorns of sin and kept from stumbling over the stones of error when we are occupied with the Gospel of peace. To be busy walking for God and bringing the message of salvation to others is a sure way to keep from sin. "How beautiful . . . are the feet of him that bringeth good tidings."

The shield of faith. This is living faith in the living God, that begins by receiving Christ as our personal Saviour. This faith believes God's promises and calls upon Him for help; this faith obeys Him.

The sword of the Spirit, which is the Word of God. Just as Christ used the Scriptures to put the Devil to flight, so we can thrust through the enemy with Bible verses that we have committed to memory. "Thy word have I hid in mine heart, that I might not sin against thee" (Ps. 119:11).

The helmet of salvation. Salvation is not only for the soul; it is also for the mind. "Casting down imaginations . . . and bringing into captivity every thought to the obedience of Christ" (II Cor. 10:5).

Praying always. This is one of the strongest weapons against Satan. It does not say, "praying sometimes, or praying when in trouble, or praying when I need something," but *praying always.* "Continue in prayer, and watch in the same with thanksgiving" (Col. 4:2). The only way Satan can touch us with his fiery darts is when we let down the armor of God, *and allow self to take over.*

V. Real Victory Over Temptation

"Now unto him that is able to keep you from falling, and to present you faultless before the presence of his glory with exceeding joy, To the only wise God our Saviour, be glory and majesty, dominion and power, both now and ever. Amen" (Jude 24).

"For in that he himself hath suffered being tempted, he is able to succor them that are tempted" (Heb. 2:18). "For we have not a high priest which cannot be touched with the feeling of our infirmities; but was in all points tempted like as we are, yet without sin" (Heb. 4:15).

"Now thanks be unto God, which always causeth us to triumph in Christ" (II Cor. 2:14).

"THAT IS VICTORY"

When you are content with any food, any raiment, any climate, any society, any solitude, any interruption by the will of God—*that is victory.*

When your good is evil spoken of, when your wishes are crossed, your taste offended, your advice disregarded, and you take it all in loving silence—*that is victory.*

When death and life are both alike to you through Christ, and you can throw all your sufferings on Jesus, and say with the apostle Paul: "Christ shall be magnified in my body, whether it be by life, or by death" (Phil. 1: 20) —*that is victory*.

Victory centers wholly in the Lord Jesus Christ. When you are wholly taken up with Him, then victory is guaranteed!

QUESTIONS

1. What proof do we have that Satan is a real person? (Eph. 2:2; John 12:31; Matt. 13:19, 39; John 13:2; II Cor. 4:4; I Tim. 3:7; I Peter 5:8, 9)
2. How do we know that Satan is limited in power and knowledge? (Job 1; Matt. 14:1-10)
3. What is Satan's one act of creation? (Ezek. 28:13-15; Isa. 14:12-15)

4. Does Satan have a kingdom? (Col. 1:13; Luke 11:14-18)

5. How does temptation come to men? (James 1:14, 15)

6. Why does the Christian have a battle within his heart? (Rom. 7:15, 19)

7. What ways does Satan use to tempt men? (I John 2:16)

8. How did Satan tempt Eve? (Gen. 3:1-6)

9. Who is greater than Satan? (I John 4:4)

10. What was the work of Christ? (I John 3:8; II Cor. 2:14)

11. What part does the Christian take when tempted? (Eph. 4:27; James 4:7; I John 5:18; Ps. 1:1, 2; Matt. 26:41; Ps. 119:11; II Cor. 10:5; Col. 4:2)

12. Is temptation ever too great for one? (I Cor. 10:13)

13. What is the provision God has made to help overcome temptation? (Eph. 6:11-18)

14. What is the result of yielding to temptation? (James 1:15)

15. What does God call those who reject Him? (Rom. 1:22)

16. What is the remedy for womankind's sin, as well as man's sin? (I Tim. 2:13-15)

17. Why does not the Christian want to practice sin? (I John 3:9)

18. How can a Christian keep right with God? (I John 1:7)

19. Why can Christ understand our temptations? (Heb. 4:15)

20. Can a Christian glorify God no matter what comes? (Phil. 1:20)

THE WILL OF GOD IN JUDGMENT

JUDGMENT MUST COME. God has no desire to wreak vengeance upon man, but guilty sinners have asked for judgment because of their rebellion and sin, and in His holiness God can never overlook sin. "For thou art not a God that hath pleasure in wickedness: neither shall evil dwell with thee. The foolish shall not stand in thy sight: thou hatest all workers of iniquity" (Ps. 5:4, 5)

The judgment upon sin has already been pronounced, for "it is appointed unto men once to die, but after this the judgment" (Heb. 9:27). "The wages of sin is death" (Rom. 6:23). "The soul that sinneth, it shall die" (Ezek. 18:4). God will never go back on His pronouncement, for He cannot lie; the death sentence must be carried out. "Tribulation and anguish, upon every soul of man that doeth evil" (Rom. 2:9).

Before we discuss some of the different judgments spoken of in Scripture, however, we shall briefly review the coming events of prophecy so we will know just where the judgments fit into the future. This will be only a skeleton review since the subject has already been covered in more detail in the preceding book, *God's Word Made Plain*.

I. Coming Events According to Prophecy

We are now living in the Age of Grace, or the Church Age, that began with the Day of Pentecost and will close with the second coming of Christ.

The coming again of Christ will be in two events. Both are called the second coming. Christ's first coming was as a Babe in Bethlehem to be the Saviour of the souls of mankind; His second coming will be to save the bodies of believers and take them to be with Him, and to establish His earthly kingdom.

The first event of the second coming of Christ is called *the rapture*, because He comes with a shout and the trumpet sound in the clouds in the air, and the believers are caught up to be with Him (I Thess. 4:13-18). No one will see Him on the earth; the saints meet Him in the air (I Cor. 15:51-53). The bodies of the Christians who have already died will be resurrected. This is the first resurrection. There will be no warning when Christ comes again in the rapture, except the signs of the times as seen in world conditions (Matt. 24:36-42; 25:13).

In passing it might be well to look at the parable which Christ told to bring out certain important warnings in connection with His coming to catch away His Church, the believers. Turn, if you will, to Matthew 25:1-13. First, though, remember that parables are earthly stories with heavenly meanings, and they are purposed to bring out some special truth but do not always necessarily carry out doctrinally in all details. This is true in this story also, although this parable is referring primarily to Israel.

"Then shall the kingdom of heaven be likened unto ten virgins." It is well to notice that the term "kingdom of heaven" does not necessarily refer to Heaven nor to the Kingdom Age of Christ; instead it applies to Christen-

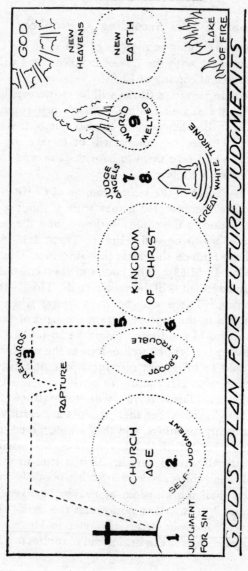

GOD'S PLAN FOR FUTURE JUDGMENTS

dom, or the time and area in which Christ is known. So often in the parables about the kingdom of Heaven we find that there are good and bad; the wheat and the tares; the good king and the enemy, etc. In other words, the kingdom of Heaven in this parable refers to the professing saints, those who know about Christ. The "kingdom of God" usually means "salvation, or belonging to the King, and the promise of Heaven." The "kingdom of Christ" refers to the Millennium, or the Kingdom Age, when Christ will reign on the earth.

Now, it is important to discern between actual interpretation and application. The parable of the ten virgins was given to the Jews especially and refers to the believers and professing believers during the Great Tribulation especially. However, it can be applied to our day as well.

"Ten virgins, which took their lamps, and went forth to meet the bridegroom" (Matt. 25:1-13). It is an Oriental custom to meet the coming celebrity. All these virgins have lamps. The lamp could not represent salvation, for some of them are not saved. It must stand for their profession, their testimony, or their religous trend. They are all *professing* believers. But only some of them are *possessing* believers.

"Five of them were wise, and five were foolish. They that were foolish took their lamps, and took no oil with them: But the wise took oil in their vessels with their lamps." In connection with salvation, oil is often a type of the Holy Spirit. A true believer has the Spirit. "Now if any man have not the Spirit of Christ, he is none of his" (Rom. 8:9). This distinguishes between the truly saved and the merely religious people.

"While the bridegroom tarried, they all slumbered and slept." It is not only the unsaved who are asleep, even

"The Wise and Foolish"

WHICH ARE YOU?

the true believers are also "sleeping at the switch." We can apply this to our day as well. God challenges us: "Awake to righteousness, and sin not; for some have not the knowledge of God: I speak this to your shame" (I Cor. 15:34). "Let us not sleep, as do others; but let us watch and be sober" (I Thess. 5:6). This is one of the signs of the last days of the Church age: that there will be coldness and laxness in spiritual sleep.

"And at midnight there was a cry made, Behold the bridegroom cometh; go ye out to meet him." Midnight is the darkest hour. If ever the world were in a midnight hour, it is today! What a preview of the darkness during the Great Tribulation! The coming of the Lord is the only solution for the chaos and confusion that are rampant throughout the whole world now, even as His coming at the end of the Tribulation will be the answer for those days.

"For the Lord himself shall descend from heaven with a shout, with the voice of the archangel" (I Thess. 4:16).

"In the moment, in the twinkling of an eye at the last trump: for the trumpet shall sound, and the dead shall be raised" (I Cor. 15:52).

"Then all those virgins arose, and trimmed their lamps." Perhaps the wicks had to be trimmed and cut. "And the foolish said unto the wise, Give us of your oil; for our lamps are gone out." No one can supply salvation for another. This is something each person must accept for himself. The Spirit is given to each one who

receives Christ, but "none of them can by any means redeem his brother, nor give to God a ransom for him" (Ps. 49:7). The term *gone out* has the meaning of "will not burn," or "has no light." A wick will not burn long without oil!

The wise virgins send the foolish to "buy for your-

selves." Unfortunately, when Christ comes there will be
no time for repentance or preparation. "And while they
went to buy, the bridegroom came." Sad, sad, their plight!
"And they that were ready [who had the Holy Spirit]
went in with him to the marriage: and the door was
shut." It reminds one of the Flood when Noah and his

The Door was shut

family went into the ark, and the people laughed at him
in scorn and derision. But when the water came down
from the heavens and came up from the fountains of the
deep below, then perhaps they rushed to the ark and
pounded on the door with the cry, "Let us in! Let us in!"
but Noah could not open the door, for God *had shut him
in!* It was too late!

When those foolish virgins cried for admittance, they
called Him, "Lord, Lord!" However, even as today when
many people call Christ "Lord" when He is not their
Lord at all, so in that day "he answered and said, Verily
I say unto you, I know you not." Scripture says, "The

Lord knoweth them that are his" (II Tim. 2:19). Christ never says to His saints, "I know you not." So these in this parable are unbelievers; they are religious, but lost.

God's warning for those in the Great Tribulation before He comes to set up His kingdom, is the same for us today, "Watch therefore, for ye know neither the day nor the hour wherein the Son of man cometh."

All the signs of the times have already been fulfilled, so that the next event of prophecy could be the Lord's return. Then it is that *all* believers will be taken away from the earth, and only unbelievers will be left to carry on through the seven years of the Great Tribulation that shall come on the earth. Satan is let loose with all his evil to give power to his Antichrist, who will become a political, religious and economic dictator over the whole world. Those who turn to God during this tribulation will be killed, for Satan's Christ will make himself as God and force all men to worship him. It is during this terrible time that the judgments of God are poured out on a rebellious world (as described in Rev. 6, 8, 9, 11, 13-18).

Scripture indicates that the believers, the Church, will not pass through this Great Tribulation, but that *all* will have been raptured to be with Christ before it begins.

A. THE CHURCH WILL NOT PASS THROUGH THE GREAT TRIBULATION

God has said that all who live godly will suffer persecution, and that all who love Him will have tribulation in this world, but this does not refer to the Great Tribulation.

1. Luke 21:36: "Watch ye therefore, and pray always, that ye may be accounted worthy to escape all these

things that shall come to pass, and to stand before the Son of man." Because we are believers, we know that we shall stand before Christ, but we long to *be worthy* of the privilege of escaping the tribulation that shall come which is described in this chapter.

2. I Cor. 15:51: "We shall not all sleep [die], but we shall *all* be changed, in a moment, in the twinkling of an eye, at the last trump: for the trumpet shall sound, and the dead shall be raised incorruptible, and we shall be changed." These words are spoken to the believers, the Church. Christ's Church is a unit and represented as His Body, His Bride. When Christ comes to take His Bride, His Body, He certainly will take *all* of it.

3. Rev. 2:22: Here the false church is warned that it will have to go through the Great Tribulation, but in Revelation 3:10 the faithful church is promised that it will not go through this Tribulation.

4. II Thess. 2:7, 8: The presence of the Holy Spirit in the Church today is keeping back the power of Satan. When He is taken out of the way at the coming of Christ when the Church is raptured, *"then shall that wicked be revealed."* So the Antichrist will not be revealed until the Church is taken away.

5. Dan. 12:1: The promise in this verse is to those whose names are written in the Book of Life. "And there shall be a time of trouble, such as never was since there was a nation even to that same time: and at that time thy people shall be delivered, every one that shall be found written in the book."

6. Rev. 4, 5: After the description of the churches given in chapters 2 and 3, which coincide exactly with the periods of church history since Christ, the apostle John in his vision heard as it were the voice "of a trumpet talking with me; which said, Come up hither, and I will

show thee things which must be hereafter. And immediately I was in the spirit: and, behold, a throne was set in heaven" (Rev. 4:1, 2).

Since the Book of Revelation is a symbolic book, this sounds very much like a symbolic preview of the rapture when John was caught up into Heaven in the spirit to come before the throne, and to see what was going on in Heaven while the woes were being poured out upon the earth. So after the Church Age, the believers will be caught up at the trumpet sound to stand before the throne of Christ, and be given spiritual bodies.

7. Rom. 5:9: "We shall be saved from wrath through him." Very certainly the Great Tribulation is part of the wrath of God, just as the last judgment is the wrath of God and the lake of fire is the wrath of God, all reserved for those who have not been saved *through Christ*. No believer will have to stand the wrath of God; that is one of the sure promises of salvation.

8. Rev. 19: The first part of this chapter shows that the saints are already with Christ in Heaven, enjoying the marriage glory and clothed in white robes. In verse 14, when Christ comes to the earth to set up His kingdom and defeat the Antichrist, the saints come with Him. Therefore they must have been taken away prior to His coming to the earth at this second part of His second coming.

It is after the seven years of the Great Tribulation that Christ returns to the earth in what is called *the revelation*. This time He comes *with* His saints, not to *take* them to Heaven; this time He comes to the earth, and not just in the air; this time every eye will see Him and there is warning just when He will come (Zech. 14; Rev. 19:11-21; II Thess. 1:7-10; Rev. 1:7; Matt. 24:29-31).

This event of Christ's coming could never be identified

with the first event of His coming when conditions are very different. It is only when these two events are clearly divided can prophecy become clear and simple.

Now it is that the Antichrist is damned into the lake of fire, and Christ sets up His kingdom on the earth with His headquarters in Jerusalem. Now it is that Israel will realize the promises made to Abraham that they shall occupy the promised land and once again be the chosen people of the King (Zech. 14).

This reign of Christ is called the Kingdom Age, or the Millennium, for it will last one thousand years and be a time of peace and plenty and prosperity. The curse on man and nature will be lifted and the lion and the lamb will play together, and they shall not learn war any more (Rev. 20:4-6; Isa. 2:1-5; 35; 60:1-22).

After this reign of Christ comes the resurrection of unbelievers and the last judgment of the Great White Throne of God.

Following this, the earth is melted with fervent heat, and God will make a new heaven and a new earth wherein dwelleth righteousness (II Peter 3:10-13).

B. THE JUDGMENTS

Now that we have given this quick view of future events, perhaps the different judgments will better fit into place as we consider each in turn.

1. The Judgment of Believers' Sins

Yes, judgment must come *but,* and how wonderful that there is a *but!* God in His mercy and love has provided One who will take the judgment for those who receive Him as their Saviour. This judgment for sin took place nineteen hundred years ago on the cross of Calvary. Our death sentence was executed upon the sinless Son of God. For he [God] hath made him [Christ] to be sin for

us, who knew no sin; that we might be made the right-eousness of God in him" (II Cor. 5:21).

Christ became the sin-bearer for the sins of the whole world. "Who his own self bare our sins in his own body on the tree [cross], that we, being dead to sins, should live unto righteousness: by whose stripes ye were healed" (I Peter 2:24).

Jesus Christ was the Substitute for the guilty sinner; the death He took was the death that we deserve; the pain He endured was the pain that we should suffer; the shame that He bore was the shame that we have earned. "Christ died for our sins."

"But we see Jesus, who was made a little lower than the angels for the suffering of death . . . that he by the grace of God should taste death for every man" (Heb. 2:9).

But the question is asked, How could the few hours that Christ spent on the cross be equivalent to an eternity in Hell, which is the penalty for sin?

The answer is best understood when we realize that Christ was *God* Himself. He is the Holy One, the sinless One; He cannot bear the presence of sin. As God, He lives in the eternal present; there is no past or future with Him. As God, He is the all-powerful One; He can do all things and He made all men. And yet; this is the God who came down to earth and allowed sinful men to crucify Him, to spit upon Him and ridicule Him! This is the One who became the bearer of the sins of the world, your sins and mine! This is the One who cried out, "My God, my God, why hast thou forsaken me?"

For the almighty, holy and eternal Son of God to bear the burden of sin even for a few hours was equivalent to an eternity in Hell for human beings!

But this is past history. This judgment for sin took place about A.D. 30. The death penalty has been paid. Now salvation and justification are offered to all who will receive Christ as their own personal Saviour. "He that believeth on him is not condemned: but he that believeth not is condemned already" (John 3:18). The whole matter hinges on the one phrase, "whosoever *believeth in him . . .* he that *believeth on him.*" Always it is the sinner's part to *accept* the remedy; otherwise the provision is to no avail. A river of fresh water does no good to a thirsty man until he drinks of it; a hearty meal does no good to a hungry man until he eats of it; a sure medicine does no good to a dying man until he takes it. So the pardon for sin is to no avail until we *receive Christ.*

While our family were prisoners of the Japanese in concentration camps, we faced the pangs of hunger especially during the last months of starvation just before liberation. We saw the bowls of steaming food that the Japanese guards were eating, we smelled the fragrance

of cooking, but it did us no good! We believed in food allright, but we could not partake of it.

But on that glorious week of liberation when the American First Cavalry came in through the very streets of Manila and set us free, they brought with them cases of canned milk, bags of rice and sugar. That next morning when we were given all the rice porridge we could eat, and as much sugar as we needed, and a can of milk to each internee, it was a day to remember! We ate with relish that has seldom been duplicated since! The strength and life began to return to our emaciated bodies. It was the eating that did the good; not just believing in food!

When we receive Christ as our water of life, our bread of life, our remedy for sin, then comes the wonderful promise that we have eternal life and shall never come into judgment. "For Christ also hath once suffered for sins, the just for the unjust, that he might bring us to God" (I Peter 3:18).

Now all the promises of safety from the last judgment are for us! "There is therefore now no condemnation to them which are in Christ Jesus" (Rom. 8:1). (In passing, it is well to note that the last phrase of that verse is not found in the earlier manuscripts, but belongs in verse 4 where it fits in the context.)

Here again, however, note the important phrase, "them which are *in* Christ Jesus." This is the clue to the whole truth. Those who are in Christ are exempt from the wrath of God. Christ says: "Verily, verily, I say unto you, He that heareth my word, and believeth on him that sent me, *hath* everlasting life, and *shall not* come into condemnation; but *is passed* from death unto life" (John 5:24).

The first judgment took place at Calvary. It meant death for Christ, but justification for the sinner from the wrath of the Great Tribulation, from the last judgment and from the lake of fire. "Being now justified by his blood, we shall be saved from wrath through him" (Rom. 5:9). Praise God!

2. *The Self-judgment of Believers*

The moment we start our Christian life by receiving Christ as Saviour is the moment we begin our day-by-day and hour-by-hour searching of our lives and the judging of daily sins. "Let a man examine himself . . . for if we would judge ourselves, we should not be judged" (I Cor. 11:28, 31). This is not speaking about civic or government judgments, but rather the confessing and forsaking of our daily sins before God. To judge our sins means to admit it is sin, hate it and put it away as we ask God for forgiveness. When we judge our own sins, God will not have to discipline us.

In I Corinthians 11, the warning is given in connection with taking the Lord's Supper without preparing our

TAKE A GOOD LOOK IN THE MIRROR OF SELF-JUDGMENT

hearts by self-examination and confession of sin. But it is also true that whenever we come into the presence of God we must confess and forsake sin, so that we might come boldly to the throne of grace to find help and mercy. This judgment should be done any time and anywhere and constantly, as our heart condemns us for ill-temper, pride, selfishness, untruth, or anything that dishonors our Lord and grieves the Holy Spirit.

However, when we receive the judgment of God upon our daily sin, it is not the judgment of lost souls. The word "damnation" in verse 29 simply means "judgment" and is explained in verse 32. "But when we are judged, we are chastened of the Lord, that we *should not* be condemned with the world." Believers will never be condemned with the lost world, but their chastening is explained in verse 30: "For this cause many are weak and sickly among you, and many sleep."

There are five results of sin in the life of a Christian, and none of them is the last judgment:

a. God will not answer prayer (Ps. 66:18; Isa. 59:1, 2). The only prayer the heavenly Father will hear from an erring child is the prayer for forgiveness. Then, and only then, is the prayer connection restored and blessing can ensue.

b. God allows trouble and sorrow to "spank" His wayward child (Ps. 32:4, 5). Physical weakness and sickness are often a loving Father's way of saying He loves us enough to discipline us so that He might bring about repentance and restoration. Usually when a Christian dies, we believe that his work is done and he has gone to

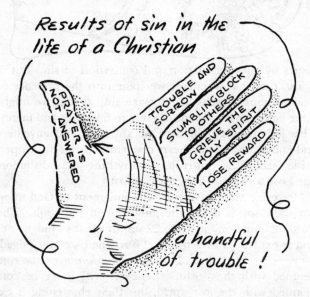

Results of sin in the life of a Christian —

PRAYER IS NOT ANSWERED

TROUBLE AND SORROW

STUMBLINGBLOCK TO OTHERS

GRIEVE THE HOLY SPIRIT

LOSE REWARD

a handful of trouble !

his reward in Heaven. Praise God, this is indeed very often the case! But sometimes it is not so. It might be that the believer's testimony is so poor that God must remove him from the earth lest he should cause others to stumble. This is what Scripture refers to as the "sin unto death" (I John 5:16), and what I Corinthians 11:30 means when it says, "and many sleep." Yes, they are still children of God, and they "die in the Lord" and will be resurrected at the first resurrection when Christ returns for His saints; nothing will change this fact. But they will lose their reward in Heaven and they grieve the heart of God.

c. A believer out of fellowship with his Lord is a stumblingblock to others (Mal. 2:8; I Cor. 9:12). The world is watching the Christian; we are the only Bible the careless world will read. The reason that many people are not interested in the Word of God today is because professing Christians are not practicing what they preach, and the world does not want what we say we have, nor like what we say we are. "But if our gospel be hid, it is hid to them that are lost" (II Cor. 4:3). No man lives unto himself, and when one Christian backslides he hinders the entire Gospel message, is a grievance to the entire church, and a poor advertisement to the world. "And whether one member suffer, all the members suffer with it" (I Cor. 12:26).

d. A believer out of fellowship with his Lord is grieving the heart of God (Eph. 4:30; Mark 3:5). The Father-heart of God longs for His children to love and obey Him so that He might bless them. It grieves Him to have to discipline us. If there were no other reason for self-judgment, this should be enough. It should be our ultimate aim to gladden the heart of God, and glorify His name.

e. A believer out of fellowship with his Lord will lose his reward when he gets to Heaven. Years of backsliding will wipe out the reward that might have been ours if we had remained faithful. Since the reward in Heaven

There are many

LISTENERS;

many

LOOKERS;

many

LOAFERS

but ~ ~ ~

LABORERS ARE FEW !

Are you a laborer, ~ or ?

will be an eternal reward, then the loss of reward will mean an eternal loss. Our status in eternity depends on our faithfulness here on earth.

Self-judgment, constantly and conscientiously, will avoid all these sad results of sin, and bring joy in Heaven as well as bring souls to the Saviour. "Restore unto me the joy of thy salvation. . . . Then will I teach transgressors thy ways; and sinners shall be converted unto thee" (Ps. 51:12, 13).

Salvation is a present possession, but rewards are a future possession.

3. *The Judgment of the Works of Believers*

"For we shall all stand before the judgment seat of Christ. . . . So then every one of us shall give account of himself to God" (Rom. 14:10, 12). "For we must all appear before the judgment seat of Christ; that every one may receive the things done in his body, according to that he hath done, whether it be good or bad" (II Cor. 5:10).

These verses are written to believers. This judgment is to test the deeds of the Christians and to give rewards to those who have been faithful, and takes place in Heaven during the Tribulation period on the earth. It is called the Judgment Seat of Christ in contrast to the last judgment, which is distinguished as the Judgment Seat of God. True, Christ is God, and He will be the Judge at both judgments, but the purpose is entirely diverse in the two events, even as the ones judged are different. All who come before the Judgment Seat of Christ are believers, and the motive for doing good deeds is given, "Knowing therefore the terror of the Lord, we persuade men" (II Cor. 5:11). Even though God is a God of love, yet He is still a God of justice and wrath. Our job is to warn men to flee from the wrath to come.

The Christian life is likened to a building that is being built upon the foundation of faith in Christ (I Cor. 3:11-15). Upon this foundation each of us is building deeds of obedience to God or we are building deeds of selfishness and disobedience. "Now if any man build upon this foundation gold, silver, precious stones, wood, hay, stubble; Every man's work shall be made manifest: for the day [the day when Christ comes] shall declare it."

The testing of our works takes place in Heaven at the Judgment Seat of Christ. It is certainly not the last judgment of unbelievers nor is it any such manmade invention as purgatory, etc. All who come to this testing are believers for they are built upon the foundation of faith in Christ.

Since the record of this judgment is symbolic (foundation, gold, silver, etc.), so the fire of testing is also symbolic, and refers to God's discernment and not to the literal fire of Hell or the imaginary fire of purgatory.

"It shall be revealed by fire; and the fire shall try every man's work of what sort it is." Everything will be naked and open before the eyes of God and all Heaven. Christ said: "But I say unto you, That every idle word that men shall speak, they shall give account thereof in the day of judgment" (Matt. 12:36). "Knowing that whatsoever good thing any man doeth, the same shall he receive of the Lord" (Eph. 6:8).

If the believer's life has been glorifying to God, he shall receive a reward. Salvation is a gift, but rewards are earned. If he has not been faithful in his Christian life, he will suffer loss. Just what that loss will mean we can never fully appreciate now, but it is clear that we shall fully understand throughout eternity when we shall have a mind that can understand all things from God's standpoint and can really comprehend just how terrible our neglect and sin have been. Then, how small will seem the activities we think so important now! How insignificant the ambitions and aims that govern our lives now! How sinful the neglect of souls, that we seem to practice every day!

When we are saved, we are saved indeed, but we shall suffer loss. "Be not deceived; God is not mocked: for whatsoever a man soweth, that shall he also reap. For he that soweth to his flesh [selfishness] shall of the flesh reap corruption [rottenness and failure]; but he that soweth to the Spirit shall of the Spirit reap life everlasting. And let us not be weary in well doing: for in due season we shall reap, if we faint not" (Gal. 6:7-9). How we should labor and pray that we may hear His "well done" when we see Him!

Christ tells of the joy in Heaven when He will commend and reward His saints. "His Lord said unto him, Well done, thou good and faithful servant: thou hast been faithful over a few things, I will make thee ruler over many things: enter thou into the joy of thy Lord" (Matt. 25:21). And again, "Well, thou good servant: because thou hast been faithful in a very little, have thou authority over ten cities" (Luke 19:17).

The Scripture indicates that there will be crowns as well as rulership. These crowns, of course, do not have to be literal items of gold, but rather some form of eternal reward for faithfulness. Revelation 4 tells of those in Heaven who are clothed in white raiment and who wear gold crowns on their heads. It also tells of the glorious worship in Heaven when those persons cast their crowns at the feet of their Lord, saying: "Thou art worthy, O Lord, to receive glory and honor and power: for thou hast created all things."

What a glorious day that will be when we shall stand before Him to hear His "well done" and to receive our crowns, *and* to have something to give back to Him in thanksgiving for all He has done for us!

Scripture mentions several crowns that believers may earn.

a. The crown of *life*.

James 1:12. The literal meaning in this verse is "the crowning of their life," and refers to that crowning day when we shall receive rewards for how we have endured suffering and testings and trials for the Lord. The secret of enduring is found in the words, "to them that *love him*." It was love for the Lord that enabled the martyrs to face death at the stake; it is love for the Lord that sends missionaries out to foreign lands to labor and die; it is love for the Lord that will give us courage to stand rebuffs and unpopularity for the name of Christ. This martyr's crown is mentioned again: "Be thou faithful unto death, and I will give thee a crown of life" (Rev. 2:10).

b. The crown of *righteousness*

This crown is for those who look for Christ's return and love His appearing (II Tim. 4:9). Here again we have the secret for success, "*love* his appearing." To look for His return means to occupy till He comes, to labor for Him, to bring in the last souls that shall be saved so that He may return. This is a crown that everyone of us may earn.

c. The crown of *glory*

I Peter 5:1-4. The crown here is for those who faithfully minister the Word of God to others. The soul-winner, the pastor, the evangelist, the missionary, all shall shine throughout eternity. "And they that be wise shall shine as the brightness of the firmament; and they that turn many to righteousness as the stars forever and ever" (Dan. 12:3). Yes, there will be many thrills when we get to glory, but one of them will be to see those whom we have won to Christ! Then how sinful will

seem the bickerings that have kept us from friendship
and fellowship with our fellow men and neighbors and
relatives, and how we will wish that we had loved them
to Christ in spite of any unfair treatment or unkindness
they might have shown toward us!

d. The crown of *rejoicing*

"For what is our hope, or joy, or crown of rejoicing?
Are not even ye in the presence of our Lord Jesus Christ
at his coming? For ye are our glory and joy" (I Thess.
2:19, 20). This ties in closely with the crown of glory,
for the apostle Paul counts his converts as his crown of
glory. We too may earn this crown, and may have the
joy of many jewels in that crown.

But just what will our crown be like that we cast at
the feet of the Lord Jesus? Will it be barren, or filled
with gems; or will there be a crown at all?

e. The *victor's* crown (the *incorruptible* crown)

"Know ye not that they which run in a race run all,
but one receiveth the prize? So run, that ye may obtain.
And every man that striveth for the mastery is temperate
in all things. Now they do it to obtain a corruptible
crown; but we an incorruptible" (I Cor. 9:24, 25). The
crown that God gives will never fade away throughout
all eternity. The victor's crown is for those who have
put away sins and hindrances so that they might glorify
God. "Let us lay aside every weight, and the sin which
doth so easily beset us, and let us run with patience the
race that is set before us, Looking unto Jesus" (Heb.
12:1, 2).

On that day when we stand before our Lord, how we
will grieve that we did not live for eternity instead of
for the pleasures of the world! How we will wish that
we had spent more time for God and less for sinful
pleasures! How we will hang our heads in shame that

our worldly habits were too strong for us, and that we did not put them away! In the light of eternity, how dim will appear the glitter of the baubles of earthly riches; how short-lived will be the success we have had in society or the arts or sports! "Bodily exercise profiteth little: but godliness is profitable unto all things, having promise of the life that now is, and of that which is to come" (I Tim. 4:8).

As a young person I lived for two things, athletics and drawing. I'm afraid that my high school and college days were highlighted by decorating for banquets, painting posters, and winning tennis games rather than studies or spiritual interests. Now as an older person, I look back and wish I had spent more time in studies and in spiritual efforts and would have more to show for those days now, and certainly more to show throughout eternity!

What a contrast are all these crowns that are available to believers to the crown of thorns that was forced on the brow of our Lord! He wore a crown of thorns that we might wear a crown of glory! "The soldiers platted a crown of thorns, and put it on his head . . . Then came Jesus forth, wearing the crown of thorns" (John 19:2-5). The wonderful part of it all is that the One who died for us and gives us the power to live for Him is also the One who rewards us for what we have done for Him! What a gracious Lord!

4. *The Judgment of the Jews*

The judgment upon unrepentant Israel is really more of a process than one event. To Abraham was given the promise that his descendants should dwell in their own land and know the blessing of God as His chosen people. These descendants are called Hebrews, Jews (taken from the name Judah), Israelites (taken from the name given to Jacob), but all down through history because these

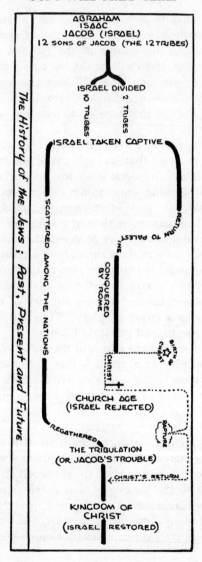

chosen people disregarded the will of God they have been tossed and scattered throughout the nations in God's judgment. The twelve tribes of Israel are descendants of the twelve sons of Jacob.

To begin with, the people quarreled so greatly among themselves that they divided into two kingdoms, and eventually were taken into captivity among the Gentile nations. During the time of Ezra and Nehemiah, two tribes returned to the land of Palestine, and it was later that Rome overcame and occupied the promised land. Christ was born during the Roman regime and His death was the Roman method of crucifixion.

After they rejected their Messiah, and crucified the Son of God, the Jews were again scattered among the Gentile nations and their land became barren and continued overtrodden by Gentile. The Scriptures prophesied that during the last days of this Age of Grace they would be regathered as a nation and return to their own land of Palestine. This has come to pass, and is one of the signs of the times that we are even now in the last days of this age.

But unbelieving Israel's greatest trouble is yet to come. After the Church is raptured, and the Antichrist takes over the world, the Jews will believe that he is their Messiah and believe his promises and covenants with them for a short time. But after three and a half years of false peace, the Antichrist will show his true colors and force the world to worship him. Then it is that the Jews will realize that he is not their Christ, and the persecutions that follow are almost unimaginable and can only be described by the chapters of the Book of Revelation, which tell of the deeds of the Antichrist and the judgments of God poured out on the earth. It is during the last half of this Great Tribulation that Israel will turn to God, and there will be a world revival in protest against the Antichrist. The Jews themselves will be the revivalists (Rev. 11), and a great number of Gentile people will turn to God, as well as the symbolic number of 144,000 of the twelve tribes of Israel (Rev. 7). Then Matthew 24:14 will be fulfilled and every tribe and nation and people will hear the Gospel.

However, many who turn to Christ during those years will be martyred by the false prophet who officiates at the worship of the Antichrist (Rev. 13). This time of tribulation is called "Jacob's trouble" (Jer. 30:3-7; Ezek. 20:34-38), and is all a part of God's judgment upon His rebellious chosen people, the Jews.

No wonder, then, that when Christ Himself does return to the earth to set up His kingdom, Israel will accept Him as their Messiah and King, and will mourn because they crucified Him. "And I will pour upon the house of David, and upon the inhabitants of Jerusalem, the spirit of grace and of supplications: and they shall look on me whom they have pierced, and they shall mourn for him, as one mourneth for his only son" (Zech. 12:10). "Behold he cometh with clouds; and every eye shall see him, and they also which pierced him: and all kindreds of the earth shall wail because of him" (Rev. 1:7).

5. The Judgment of the Antichrist

At the end of the Great Tribulation, the Antichrist will gather his armies together against Jerusalem for the Battle of Armageddon, and when the armies are in array, Christ returns to the earth to defeat Satan's Christ, and set up His own kingdom for a thousand years. The Antichrist and his false prophets are condemned into the lake of fire, and the birds of the air are filled with the flesh of his armies that are killed by the coming of Christ (Rev. 19:11-21; II Thess. 2:8).

The believers will come back with Christ at His revelation, and will reign with Him a thousand years, according to their faithfulness here in this life.

6. The Judgment of the Gentile Nations

Matthew 25:31-46. Here is a much misunderstood passage of Scripture. Many churches seem to think that this account refers to the last judgment, and that at that time all people will be gathered before God to see if they have done good or bad. The good will be "the sheep" and go to Heaven, and the bad will be "the goats" and go to Hell. This is far from harmony with the rest of Scripture, as well as from the context of the prophecy.

To begin with, this judgment takes place on earth when Christ comes to set up His kingdom, and not after the Kingdom Age when the last judgment takes place. Next, before Him are gathered the Gentile *nations* which

SHEEP NATIONS   GOAT NATIONS

He separates as sheep and goats. This is not a judgment of individuals, but of Gentile nations, and no books are opened as in the last judgment.

Just what is the basis of division at this time? The sheep nations were those which befriended the "brethren" of Christ. But who are the brethren? Remember that this account is in the Book of Matthew, and the emphasis is on the Jews who were the chosen people of Christ's human race, His brethren according to the flesh. Before the death of Christ, the term "brethren" is applied to Christ's half-brothers (the children of Mary and Joseph) and to His earthly nation, Israel. Since the half-brothers and half-sisters of Christ have long since died, the process of elimination leaves only the race of Israel.

The "sheep" nations are those who have been kind and tolerant to Israel, and the "goat" nations are those who have persecuted Israel. The "sheep" nations do not go to Heaven in this account, but enter the Kingdom Age on earth when Christ will have His headquarters in Jerusalem. They "inherit the kingdom prepared for you" (Matt. 25:34).

7. The Judgment of Satan and Angels

This is part of the final judgment. Now comes the judgment of wicked angels when they will be cast into the lake of fire prepared for them and the Devil (Rev. 20:10). This is presided over by the believers (I Cor. 6: 3). Since nothing else is told us about this, we must leave conjecture alone, and wait till that day to understand it all. But we are told, however, which angels will be judged at this time. Satan's demons and angels as well as "the angels which kept not their first estate, but left their own habitation, he hath reserved in everlasting chains under darkness unto the judgment of the great day" (Jude 6). These appear to be the angels that sinned at the time of Noah. "For if God spared not the angels that sinned, but cast them down to hell [sheol], and delivered them into chains of darkness, to be reserved unto judgment; And spared not the old world, but saved Noah" (II Peter 2:4, 5).

The story of the Flood (Gen. 6), has suggested to some Bible teachers that there was intermarriage between angels and humans that produced a race of giants, or monstrosities, that grieved God exceedingly. Some have believed that angels are not sexless, but masculine. They do not marry since there is no need to propagate and replenish, and there are no female angels. (In fact, neither do they have wings! Only the cherubim and seraphim have wings.) Instead, the angels are manifested as men. In the Book of Job (ch. 1), we have the account of the angels appearing before God, and they are called "the sons of God." In Genesis 6:2 the same term is used. "The sons of God saw the daughters of men that they were fair; and they took them wives of all which they chose." It is in the New Testament that the term "sons of God" refers to the believers who have been born again by faith in Christ Jesus.

After the resurrection we shall be like the angels only in that we shall not marry or give in marriage, and shall not be like them in any other way.

8. *The Great White Throne—The Judgment Seat of God*

At this final judgment comes the resurrection of unbelievers from death and Hell (Sheol). They receive their resurrection bodies and stand before God (Rev. 20:11-15). This is called the second resurrection, and the judgment is not to see which will go to Heaven or Hell, but rather to pass sentence upon them as to the degree of punishment. They are judged according to their deeds

recorded in God's books, and their names are certainly not in the Book of Life. Only believers' names are written down in the Lamb's Book of Life. There is an awful blank where the names of unbelievers might have been if they had received Christ as their Saviour.

There are degrees of punishment in Hell, just as there are degrees of rewards in Heaven (Jude 13). A very special place of darkness is reserved for those who teach wrong doctrines, and lead others away from God's Word.

Thank God, no believer will ever stand before this great Judgment Seat of God! But we shall all be there to see that final judgment. Although it is such a comfort to know that we who are *in Christ* shall never come into judgment, yet how terrible to think that others will stand there condemned, to whom we have neglected to give the message of life! Then we shall fully realize our failure and the price of neglect! But then it will be too late! Neighbors and friends, family and acquaintances might stand there before God and hear the terrible sentence: "Depart . . . ye wicked . . . I never knew you." Oh, Christians! How can we waste our time and neglect the souls around us? Oh, that we might get busy for God before it is too late!

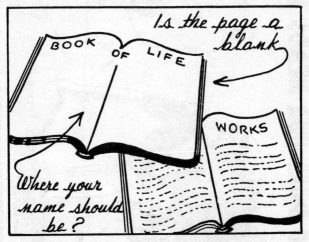

It was while we were home on furlough from the mission field that we lived near a couple that did not make a practice of going to church. I never got well acquainted with them because they used to chase our dog with threatenings, "Get your dog out of our garden, or I'll shoot him!" They had a nice garden, but we thought we had a nice dog! So we left them strictly alone.

When it came time to return to the mission field again, we sold our house and I was glad that we would not have to live near that couple any more. When we drove away from that street for the last time, I remember thinking to myself, "Well, I'm glad I won't have to see them again!" It is strange, is it not, how we think that we can

put on the robe of Christian service when we go to a
certain meeting, a certain mission field, at some certain
time, and forget that we are *always* missionaries if we are
born again!

It was some years later when I was home on furlough
again, that I picked up the newspaper one day and saw
that particular woman's name in the headlines, "Mrs. ——
Killed in Automobile Crash!" It struck me like a blow
that she was gone forever and I had never even given her
a testimony! Yes, I will see her again. If someone else
did not bring her the message of salvation, then I will
see her on that last judgment day when she may have to
stand before God condemned and I will be there to
watch. What will I have to say then? She may point her
finger at me and say, "You cared more for your children's
dog than you did for my soul!"

We do not *volunteer* to be missionaries. We are *com-
missioned* the very moment we are born again. Each of
us is assigned with the message of salvation, and no matter when or where, we can never shake the full-time responsibility we have been given to "publish glad tidings."
God says to us: "When I say unto the wicked, Thou shalt
surely die; and thou givest him not warning, nor speakest
to warn the wicked from his wicked way, to save his life:
the same wicked man shall die in his iniquity; but his
blood will I require at thine hand" (Ezek. 3:18).

Even though this last judgment is called the Judgment
Seat of God, yet it is Christ Himself who will be the
Judge (John 5:22, 23). After all, He is God, so the term
that God is the Judge is quite correct. But why is Christ
to be the Judge? Because He is the Saviour who gave His
life that men might not have to be judged! The ones
who stand before Him are those who have rejected Him
as their Saviour. Now He is no longer the Saviour, the

Advocate for their sin, but now He is the Judge. What a fearful thought! The lost will stand speechless before Him, for they will have no excuse.

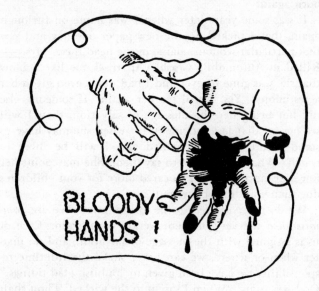

BLOODY HANDS !

A widow, who had a wild and rebellious son, was approached by a lawyer friend one day, who said, "Would you mind if I had a talk with Sam? He is growing up to be a mighty tough young man, and I fear he might get into serious trouble some day. I would like to help if I could."

"Oh," the woman exclaimed, "he's just having his fling! He's young, and he'll come out of it all right. There is good in Sammy!" So the lawyer never had an interview with Sam, and Sammy grew older and more of a problem.

Several years later there was a city-wide scandal. The

newspapers screamed the headlines, "SAM ——— AR-
RESTED FOR MURDER!"

Then the poor mother went scurrying over to her
friend the lawyer, and almost on bended knees begged
him to handle Sammy's case. "Now I accept your offer!"
she wept.

"But I'm not free to handle the case," the lawyer protested. "For since I came to you with my offer to help I
have been made a judge, and this case is to come before
me."

The case did come before that judge. Sam was found
guilty by the jury. The former friend had to pronounce
the death penalty.

Christ is still the Saviour. If you are reading these
pages and have not yet accepted Christ as your Saviour,
you have no part in justification and glory. You are still
lost and need the Saviour. Won't you receive Him now
as your personal Saviour and let Him be your Advocate
instead of your Judge? Now is the time for salvation;
then it will be too late!

A LOST SOUL SPEAKS

"Here I am in Hell! Billions of years ago I lived on
the earth and thought I was having a good time. I did
as I wanted, and I laughed and played and ate and drank,
and cared nothing about God. Now I understand the
folly of my ways; I understand how great was the salvation offered me when I was alive on earth; I understand
how wicked the errors of my sin; I understand the meaning of eternity in Hell! Here I am in unutterable tor-
ment of body and soul . . . I have no rest . . . I have no
peace . . . There is no love, for I hate everyone. There
is no hope, for this is forever and ever. My companions
are the criminals, the depraved men and women of all

history, the demons, the fallen angels and the Devil himself . . . and there is everlasting weeping and gnashing of teeth! There is not one drop of water to quench my burning thirst, there is no light, no respite from my remorse of mind. I am tormented in flames that will never consume me.

Yet now I know why I am here. I know I deserve to be here. I know too the real meaning of salvation and the glory that might have been mine. I know the meaning of all the good that I overlooked in life. I am lost, lost, lost, forever and forever. Oh, that I had heeded the warning when I could! Oh, that I had not trampled under foot the blood of the Son of God! Oh, that . . .! Oh, that . . .!"

I cannot end this book on such a note. How wonderful that we are still living in this day of grace! You still have the chance to pray right now and say, "Lord, save me!" Will you do it? Say with the hymn writer:

Just as I am, without one plea, But that Thy blood
was shed for me,
And that Thou bidd'st me come to Thee, O Lamb
of God, I come! I come!

Just as I am, and waiting not To rid my soul of one
dark blot,
To Thee, whose blood can cleanse each spot, O
Lamb of God, I come! I come!

Just as I am, tho' tossed about With many a con-
flict, many a doubt,
Fightings and fears within, without, O Lamb of
God, I come! I come!

Just as I am, poor, wretched, blind; Sight, riches,
healing of the mind,
Yea, all I need, in Thee I find, O Lamb of God,
I come! I come!

Just as I am! Thou wilt receive, Wilt welcome, pardon, cleanse, relieve;
Because Thy promise I believe, O Lamb of God, I
come! I come!

QUESTIONS

1. Why must God judge sin? (Ps. 5:4, 5)
2. What has God promised will come upon sinners?
    (Heb. 9:27; Rom. 6:23; Ezek. 18:4; Rom. 2:9)
3. What is the *rapture?* (I Thess. 4:13-18; I Cor. 15:
    51-53)
4. What is the *revelation?* (Zech. 14:1-4; Rev. 19:11-16;
    Matt. 24:29-31; Rev. 1:7)
5. Can any man redeem the soul of another? (Ps. 49:7)

6. How do we know that the five foolish virgins represent unbelievers? (Matt. 25:12)

7. How do we know that believers will not have to pass through the Great Tribulation? (Luke 21:36; I Cor. 15:51; Rev. 2:22; Dan. 12:1; Rom. 5:9)

8. What will the reign of Christ be like? (Rev. 20:4-6; Isa. 2:1-5; 35; 60:1-22)

9. What is Judgment No. 1? (I Peter 2:24; Heb. 2:9; John 5:24; Rom. 8:1)

10. What is Judgment No. 2? (I Cor. 11:28-32)

11. What is Judgment No. 3? (Rom. 14:10, 12; II Cor. 5:10; I Cor. 3:11-15)

12. What is Judgment No. 4? (Jer. 30:3-7; Ezek. 20:34-38)

13. What is Judgment No. 5? (Rev. 19:11-21; II Thess. 2:8)

14. What is Judgment No. 6? (Matt. 25:31-46)

15. What is Judgment No. 7? (Rev. 20:10; Jude 6; I Cor. 6:3)

16. What is Judgment No. 8? (Rev. 20:11-15)

17. Are Christians responsible to witness to the lost? (Ezek. 3:18)

18. What crowns may be earned by Christians? (James 1:12; II Tim. 4:8; I Peter 5:1-4; I Thess. 2:19, 20; I Cor. 9:24, 25)

19. What crown did Christ wear that we might have a crown of glory? (John 19:2-5)